FULL CIRCLE

FULL CIRCLE

A memoir of leaning in too far
and the journey back

ERIN CALLAN
MONTELLA

TRIPLE M PRESS
SANIBEL, FLORIDA

Triple M Press
Sanibel, Florida

LIBRARY OF CONGRESS IN-PUBLICATION DATA
Library of Congress Control Number: 2016903814
Montella, Erin Callan
Full Circle / Erin Callan Montella

ISBNs
978-0-9973821-0-5 (hardback)
978-0-9973821-1-2 (paperback)
978-0-9973821-2-9 (ebook)

Editing by NewYorkBookEditors.com
Cover Photo by Anthony Montella
Book Cover Design by OctagonLab.com
Interior Book Design by AuthorFriendly.com
Set in Adobe Calson Pro and Century Gothic

Printed in the United States of America

For my husband Anthony and daughter Maggie,
who complete my circle.

CONTENTS

INTRODUCTION

MY HUSBAND, ANTHONY, is a great storyteller. There is just something about his detailed recollection, the just barely believable plot line, and the buildup of drama that draws you in. Even if I've heard the same story over and over, it gets me every time. My brother-in-law Michael always jokes that when he hears Anthony's stories, he feels like he has never done anything in his life. Sometimes I feel the same way.

Somehow Anthony seems to have lived a bigger, more exciting, and sometimes more tragic life than the rest of us. There's some truth to that, but the real reason that his stories are so gripping is his confidence in what the story is, how it all fits together, the themes, the interconnectedness, the moral. I admire and envy his abilities not only because they entertain, but because they enhance his life. Anthony is one of the happiest, most optimistic people I know because everything that happens to him gets co-opted into his story line. He makes it all fit. He doesn't experience chaos and randomness. Having spent the past several years of my life with Anthony, I see that for him events, both good and bad, serve a purpose. They push him forward to finish the chapter, and each chapter builds on another to make a fully formed life. For all of us, our stories create who we are, as we choose, in our own words.

I've struggled with my own story. I think many of us do. Even putting our experiences into a framework that has logical flow is difficult, but I now know why it is critical to try to know our stories. Knowing your story means living a considered life. Socrates had it right. An unexamined life is not really worth living. Maybe that's a bit extreme, but without self-reflection, we never learn from our mistakes, condemned to repeat the same pattern over and over. But I've never had Anthony's confidence when defining my own narrative. The memories are fuzzier to me, the drama (most of the time) much less, my own engaged consciousness a fraction of what it should have been.

A few months ago I got a surprise e-mail from Shannon, an old friend from college. I was excited to hear from her and get an update about her life and kids, since we haven't seen each for more than twenty years. But even though it was a thrill to hear from her, a week after her e-mail I still hadn't written back. I was not quite sure what to say. What has really happened and what should I tell her? How do you condense twenty years of your life into an e-mail? What is my story?

Even if the critical themes of my life experience had not been clear to me, what others believe my story to be has been told based on one single and distinctive fact: I was chief financial officer of Lehman Brothers for six months straddling 2007 into 2008. A top executive during the last year of the existence of one of the oldest investment banks prior to its bankruptcy, which sent the global financial system into a tailspin. I am one of many players in the greater drama of the financial crisis whose persona has been crafted from wisps of facts. I find it almost impossible to read about that version of myself. The character in that play. It feels like she has nothing to do with me. If I have trouble knowing my story, how could anyone else possibly know it who has spent a fraction of the time on the question?

I ultimately ended up writing back to Shannon one morning soon after those thoughts rattled around my head, because in the last year something has changed. Despite more than forty-seven years of walking around in a well-established haze, I am starting to appreciate that events in my life have not been purely random and how I choose to look at them and relate them is the key to understanding my story.

In 2011, I started to try to write something about my life experiences. It seemed that there must be something worth sharing. What was it really? I couldn't quite figure it out. Anthony kept encouraging me to write stories as they occurred to me. After some time he thought I might weave them into some whole cloth. At worst, the exercise would be great therapy, forcing myself into a deeper consideration of all that happened, especially the final year of my career. I wrote things down in fits and starts for a few years with no real rhyme or reason. There were no "Aha" moments. In early March of 2013, though, I felt an overwhelming need to respond to press I was reading about Sheryl Sandberg's soon-to-be-released book *Lean In*. All of a sudden it seemed important to me to alert women to the possible hazards of devoting your entire story to your career. I was a case study in letting your career dominate your life, and it wasn't such a pretty picture. I felt so strongly that I decided to share some vulnerable information about myself and to step out into the public spotlight I had actively avoided for years. I sat down to write for about forty-five minutes and sent the short piece into the *New York Times* Op-Ed mailbox. And there it was, I had a story. It snuck up on me. I am not sure I ever put things so bluntly in casual conversation as I did in the Op-Ed piece. It felt good; it felt right.

I will admit it also scared me to death because there was such an overwhelming response to what I had written and I had guarded my privacy so carefully for years. That Monday morning, after the Sunday Op-Ed appeared, I was bombarded with phone calls, faxes, and e-mails. Many of the inquiries were from the media with interview requests and speaking invitations. There were also calls and e-mails from ordinary people thanking me for writing about my story and explaining how they related to the message. To say I was completely unprepared for such a dramatic reaction is to put it mildly. I had not anticipated putting myself back into the public eye by way of a few paragraphs in the *New York Times*. What I know, when I review the substance of the feedback, is that I struck a chord. That story made sense to tell.

CHAPTER ONE

Lines in the Sand

IN 2011 MY HUSBAND, Anthony, and I were at the NYU Fertility Center in Manhattan for our first round of in vitro fertilization, or IVF. We had been trying to have a baby for a few years, but since I was already forty-five years old, we'd conceded that we needed help. It was the most important day of the month-long cycle, the day the doctor would place the fertilized embryos back in my body after weeks of twice-daily shots, blood tests, and ultrasounds. We were ushered into a small room to wait for a doctor whom we had not met before, since the doctors in the center rotated days for the various procedures. He walked in briskly, told us his name, and got right down to business. He reviewed our legal names, dates of birth, and other information to make sure he was dealing with the right patient. We eagerly anticipated what he would tell us about the embryos, because each step up to that point had gone so well. Every measurement along the way had pointed to a much better outcome than could have been expected at my age. Because my age was what really mattered, much more than Anthony's. That's just how it is.

We listened closely. I wanted to savor the moment, so that I could repeat the dialogue verbatim back to others and remember it for a long time. The doctor let us know that he'd "seen worse" embryos than the ones he was about to implant in me. That was the sum total of his evaluation. The moment we'd waited for so anxiously. He'd "seen worse." That's it. Wow. To say we were surprised and disheartened would be an understatement. Up to that point all our results had been lights-out. We knew the probabilities were low for getting me pregnant at forty-five years old, but as Anthony always reminds me, "Someone has to be Derek Jeter." Someone has to be that person who defies the odds and has unimaginable success. We both sincerely believed that. Why not us?

After our brief and unexpectedly disappointing conversation, I had to walk alone with the doctor to the operating room. I tried to stay optimistic. I reminded myself how powerful the state of mind is for the body. As we walked slowly together, he started to ask questions, as I guess he usually does with his patients. "So what do you do?" he asked. This had always been a strange and complicated question for me since I left my career on Wall Street. But in New York, talking about jobs is an unavoidable conversation starter. "I'm retired," I said, simply. "Really? From what?" he asks. I paused a minute and tried to keep my voice as matter-of-fact as I could. "I was a banker." This was my standard response when I tried to put an end to this line of questioning. In New York City, with bankers by the thousands, that answer wasn't much of a tip-off. I certainly had no interest in talking about my job history at this moment in my life.

He keeps going. "Where did you work?" he asks, and I knew I wasn't getting off the hook. We had reached the operating room and the attending nurse had asked me to lie on the table on my back with my knees bent and spread. Always my favorite position for having a conversation. I hoped that maybe the doctor would be distracted by the medical procedure at hand, but no such luck. As I arranged my feet so embarrassingly in the stirrups, he asked me again, "Where did you work?" I had willfully turned my attention to the nurse, who was advising me about my positioning for the procedure. I tried to stay focused, because trust me, I can slip. I can get lulled right back into talking about my all-important career as if nothing else has ever mattered. I didn't want to go there, but I had to say something.

I turned back to the doctor. "Lehman Brothers," I said, as levelly as possible. He looked at me, looked down at my chart, and looked at me again. Even with the oh-so-flattering surgical hat on my head, his eyes widened a bit and then he says very deliberately and slowly, "Oh, you're *that* Erin Callan. I read all about you in *Too Big to Fail.*"

I couldn't imagine a comment I wanted to hear less as I was lying on the operating table. I was forty-five years old, trying to have a baby after spending my life focused on prioritizing my career. I have never read *Too Big to Fail*, nor have I read any similar book or article, because reading someone else's secondhand description of those events is unsettling, at best.

Unfortunately the embryo transfer procedure for IVF that I was having that day does not require anesthesia, so for several minutes I heard about the financial crisis and women in the workplace from my new doctor friend. The best I could hope for was that in some weird way maybe he thought it would be cool to have patients he had heard of, and that would make him do his best. That's probably not fair to the doctor, since I am sure he always works for the best outcome. I think I was just so focused on any little sign that this was going to work.

It was fair enough that he asked me about it. People are curious and can't help themselves. It doesn't occur to them how many others have asked before. The same thing happened to my husband, a New York City firefighter who was at the World Trade Center site on 9/11. When someone finds out he was a firefighter, they inevitably ask him about 9/11. The bankruptcy of Lehman Brothers is in no way comparable in magnitude or tragedy to 9/11, but there is a similar type of morbid curiosity when it comes to people's fascination with disaster of all kinds.

As hard as I tried to close that chapter of my life and establish my new life away from Wall Street, it always seeped back in—or sometimes crashed—when I least expected it. Sometimes I wondered why I felt the need to erase that part of my story. For years, I tried to pretend that part of my life didn't exist. It was bizarre, really, as if the previous twenty years of my life never happened. I didn't really have my story yet, at least not one I could believe in and feel good about it. That's what I needed.

"Could you handle it if things didn't work out with your job?" Anthony asked me. "Sure...why not?" I said casually, not missing a beat. I didn't pause. I didn't even consider another possible answer. It was late 2007 and Anthony, whom I had just reconnected with from high school, was asking me about work and its role in my life. In hindsight, it could have been a *New York Post* Page Six cartoon, everyone chuckling at the preposterousness of the air bubble over my head: "Sure...why not?"

It ended up that nothing could have been further from the truth. Only a year later, on the night before Christmas Eve in 2008, I would be in the emergency room of Southampton Hospital on Long Island. I had seriously tried to hurt myself. That's something very few people know. Anyone who has known me well in my life would have a hard time believing it, but I think it's important for people to know it about me. It was the ultimate act of selfishness and hopelessness. That's how far I took this whole thing.

I guess you need to be closer to the end to understand the beginning. For me, with my career, I had to be well past the end. In fact, I needed more than five years of what I consider now to be real life to make sense of the prior twenty-five. And these years since that first conversation with Anthony have been a roller coaster. Clarity. Fog. Clarity. Fog. But events build on each other even in fits and starts, and progress struggles to win out. An understanding starts to emerge. Not on the timetable I wanted, but if I know anything, I know good results take years of hard work, so why should this be any different?

So how did I get to a hospital bed on Christmas Eve in 2008? After such a seemingly accomplished and happy life, how did I lose my way so badly? The story seems complicated on the surface, but at its heart, it's shockingly simple. By the age of forty-two, I had made my career the absolute center of my existence, consuming all my energy and focus. It appeared that my dedication had paid off when I became chief financial officer of Lehman Brothers at the end of 2007. I wasn't just the highest-ranking woman on Wall Street, but one of the highest-ranking *people* on Wall Street, period. And I was proud of my job. I drank the Lehman Brothers Kool-Aid. The Reverend Jim Jones had nothing on Dick Fuld, the CEO, and Joe Gregory, the president. I believed to my core that Lehman was a special place filled with special people, and that I had a special place there. I would have been on the first plane to Jonestown.

As you read this I am sure you're wondering how I could have been so naive. I think I confused success with passion. Because I was doing so well, my career was surely what I loved. It must have been what I was meant to do with my life. I had it backward. Maybe I thought I loved it because I was so good at it. And maybe it seemed easier to be good at work than good at life.

Anthony and I had recently watched a documentary about a successful professional athlete who referred to the sport he played as his platform, not his purpose. A jumping-off point to accomplish bigger and better things. The things that mattered more in life. That simple idea that a career could be a platform, not a purpose, was like a slap across the face. The good kind. A wake-up call. I had done the opposite, making a successful career my purpose, not a platform for something more meaningful. And, really, in and of itself, my career had no purpose. I am not talking about a job, a means to survive and take care of others. I am talking about my career. The concept of career, for me, suggests a broader meaning of a life plan marrying your interests, passions, and livelihood. What meaningful goal or agenda was I accomplishing with all that effort and energy flowing into my career? My career was not a means to an end. It was the end. When I reflect on all the sacrifices that were made for that end, it strikes me as somewhat wasteful. I could have achieved a purpose with my platform, but that would have required changing my priorities and modifying my approach in ways I never would have considered at the time.

It didn't start out that way for me. I never planned to have a take-no-prisoners approach to a successful career. Maybe that's surprising, since the common assumption seems to be that successful people really know themselves and their goals. They've always had the right game plan, and everybody wants to know the secret. I have certainly had many young men and women come to me for advice over time to try to get the roadmap, the formula to get to the top. Until you're there, it's hard to accept that there isn't one. It's not like I'm holding back the secret sauce, like a fisherman protecting a favorite fishing spot, and somehow, if I let you know the information, there's less in it for me. Success is so much more random than that. And, honestly, I did know myself most of the time along the way—until I didn't. That's how it goes, and my path to the top cost me a lot along the way. This memoir includes a handful of stories so you can see how I lost my way. Lost myself. How I let work and everything that went along with it become the center of my life, defining everything about my purpose. And then, with a lot of struggle, I found myself again. I hadn't disappeared. I just went missing for a while.

When I really think about it, there were early signals of the kind of extremism I ultimately exhibited with work. Like most things, the switch rarely gets turned "on" in a single day. At a young age I figured out sooner than later how to put a stop to it. When I was thirteen years old, I had already been an avid competitive gymnast for more than five years when I made a relatively dramatic decision to quit gymnastics. Without any context this does not seem like a big deal—a kid deciding that she doesn't like a hobby anymore—but I had spent virtually every day for the seven years up to that point in time doing gymnastics. I ate, drank, slept, and even dreamed gymnastics.

I had started gymnastics at about six years old when I saw Olga Korbut in the 1972 Olympics. I was completely dazzled. After years of dedicated training, I became an extremely successful gymnast, competed nationally, and, up to the age of thirteen, spent about twenty hours a week at the gym in addition to going to school. Now it's easy to see that I was only a little kid. But at the time, it was serious. I was featured on the front page of the Sunday "Sports" section of the *New York Times*. Life revolved around the next workout. I kept a diary of my training and what I wanted to learn next. My best friends were my gymnastics teammates. I didn't go out to play after school, I went to gymnastics. I didn't eat dinner with my family a few nights a week; I ate by myself when I got home from practice late in the evening. Somehow I fit in my homework, but not much else. I gave up a normal kid life to be excellent, to be at the top of my field. The sacrifices seemed worth it. It was my thing.

When I was thirteen and about to start high school, my coaches had insisted I needed to attend high school on a part-time basis so that I could dedicate most of my days to my gymnastics training. But then I did the unthinkable. I stopped cold turkey. I decided gymnastics couldn't work in my life.

I grew up in a town called Douglaston, which is on the eastern edge of Queens County in New York City, and I was set to attend high school at St. Francis Prep in Fresh Meadows, Queens, not far from Douglaston. Despite the best efforts of my gymnastics coaches in trying to convince the administrators differently, St. Francis didn't make special school schedules for students for sports. I could conform to their schedule or go somewhere else, such as a full-time gymnastics training center in Connecticut where normal high school academics were cobbled together through full-time tutoring. But even though I had based my life around gymnastics, I knew I wanted to go to a normal high school. I wanted to ride the bus with my friends, go to football games, play sports, go to dances, and take classes filled with other kids my own age. I didn't want to live in my own little bubble of gymnastics success separated from the ordinary teenage experience. Especially since any gymnastics career is typically over by age eighteen. Then what? What was the point?

The lines were drawn hard in the sand, and I chose real life over gymnastics. Real life just seemed like it had more potential. It was such a good decision, so mature. I wish I had taken the wisdom of that experience with me when I found my life being swallowed by my career. It's strange to think that as a kid I was more aware and reasonable than I was as an adult. Of course, although the decision was the right one, the aftermath was really hard. There was a gaping hole in my life. I didn't really know who I was without gymnastics. At fourteen, I felt like I was starting over. What would I do every day? I quickly started to play tennis, a sport I had dabbled in and that could fill my time and satisfy my athletic tendencies. I ended up playing tennis competitively throughout high school. I played on my varsity high school tennis team and competed on a circuit run by the Eastern Tennis Association. I was a good natural athlete so it only took a year or so before I was a ranked junior player. I ultimately went on to play on the varsity team in college, but I didn't approach the sport of tennis with anything near the intensity of my approach to gymnastics. It was ancillary and complimentary to my life, not at the center of it. When all was said and done, the most fun I had in tennis was playing for my high school tennis team, which was the least competitive, least high-profile scenario. Tennis really isn't a team sport, but my high school tennis team was tight and I loved having teammates.

Despite that, though, I had trouble feeling truly satisfied with tennis. I wasn't obsessed and that didn't feel right. It just felt a bit half-assed, really. It is hard to deny that there were certainly a lot of positives about playing tennis, like all sports, but though I was good at it, I didn't love it. I knew I should have been glad that it didn't rule my life. That was the idea when I quit gymnastics, right? But some part of me wanted my life dominated by something. My tennis experience also fits in the category of "sometimes it's confusing to be good at something." It still may not be what you love.

At least I can see from my gymnastics decision that there I had some amount of healthy self-awareness at a young age. I had something of a sense of what was good for me, the human me who needed more than a sport to be the focus of my existence. It wasn't easy, but I'd figured out how to balance my desire for achievement with a healthy normal life. It wouldn't last. It took me thirty years to come back to this good kind of decision making, with proper life priorities that had the potential for fulfillment and happiness. It took years for the wisdom of my youth to finally return. It just shows you that your innate, primal instincts can be the right ones, before they get squeezed out by all sorts of other learned messages. Through all my extremist tendencies, I just needed to come back full circle to that thirteen-year-old girl from Douglaston, Queens, who knew herself better.

CHAPTER TWO

My Brilliant Plan

IN THE SPRING OF 1983, my senior year of high school, I had an appointment to meet with our school's college counselor to discuss the colleges that had accepted me in order to talk about next steps on making a final decision. It must have been mandatory to meet with the counselor, regardless of your circumstances, because I doubt I would have opted for the meeting voluntarily. I felt like I had the whole college topic under control. I had been attending St. Francis Prep for over three years. St. Francis was a great school and the largest Catholic school in the country. As a Catholic school, it was pretty progressive in many ways, starting with being coeducational, which was rare in Catholic schools, especially in Brooklyn and Queens. But even though it was somewhat nontraditional, it still offered a core of old-school Catholic education. The college counselor, Sister Joseph Agnes, was a nun who was seventy years old if she was a day. Appearances didn't suggest she was hip to college life in the 1980s.

This meeting was late in the process, after all the applications had been submitted and acceptances and rejections were in hand, probably sometime in late April of my senior year. I had done all my own homework on applying to schools, filling out the applications and writing the essays, so I felt prepared and reasonably educated about my options. As I sat in Sister Joseph Agnes's office and reviewed my acceptances with her, something became clear very quickly. She was a big proponent of the Catholic universities where I'd been accepted, like Notre Dame and Georgetown. She wasn't so keen on the Ivy League schools. Public enemy number one was Harvard. And, of course, going into the meeting, Harvard was where I intended to go. How could I not go to Harvard if I'd got in?

It all seemed pretty straightforward to me and I had expected her to have a similar view. I thought it would be great for our high school to have someone go to Harvard and that the school, and Sister Joseph Agnes, would see it that way. Boy, I was wrong about that. What I thought was going to be a five-minute meeting with lots of congratulations and encouragement started to drag. Sister Joseph Agnes tried to work around her message subtly at first. Inferences of atheism and godlessness were peppered in to the conversation. I wasn't sure I was hearing her right. She was a powerful force, all hundred pounds of her in her nun's habit. She had me back on my heels, and then she zeroed in for the kill. With a knowing look she leaned in and said conspiratorially, "You know, Erin, I hear that many women who go to Harvard are there to get their 'M-R-S.'" She leaned back in her seat, waiting for the lightbulb to go off in my head. I paused and thought. I'd heard of MBAs, PhDs, MAs, but what was an MRS? Then it hit me. It wasn't MRS it was "Mrs." She actually was suggesting women went to Harvard to meet men to marry.

Trying to reason with her seemed futile, but I did try. It has always been hard for me to hear obvious untruths and just let them go unchallenged. You can ask my sister Beth about that. Having shared a room with me all our growing-up years, Beth has long been used to my interrogating style. So instead of buckling down and figuring out how to get out of Sister Joseph Agnes's office quickly, I had to speak my mind.

"Sister, you think that young women work hard in high school to get great grades, be top of their class, be good athletes or musicians, or whatever else, just to get in to Harvard to meet a guy?" I asked. I had girlfriends who would go to pretty great lengths for their boyfriends, but this was ridiculous. "I can't believe that," I told her, "and it's certainly not my motivation." Well, as you can imagine, that didn't make Sister Joseph Agnes happy. I certainly didn't change her mind. I am sure her view didn't represent the institutional view of St. Francis Prep. Most of the teachers that knew me were very supportive of my choice. But whether or not they were, I knew in my own mind and knew what I wanted for myself. I didn't want anyone else to make my decisions for me.

It didn't take any great amount of self-awareness to see beyond what was some flawed guidance about college choices, even for a teenager. But it does remind me I was marching to the beat of my own drummer at that point in my life and I felt confidence in my convictions. This was a good thing. It wasn't overconfidence; not yet. That came later. It was healthy confidence.

One aspect of this memory does make me laugh, though. Sister Joseph Agnes didn't actually have it all wrong. It turned out there were a lot of young women who came to Harvard, mostly on the weekends, to get their "MRS," they just didn't go to school there. They flocked from the local women's colleges in the Boston area to meet eligible Harvard men. It created a strange dynamic, and probably made it less likely that the women who attended Harvard would end up marrying their male counterparts, I am sure it happened more than I know, but none of my friends married Harvard classmates. It just didn't work out that way.

It seems to me we are quick to look at these types of stories from a gender angle. But I don't really see the conversation with Sister Joseph Agnes as having anything to do with me being female. If I were a male student, I think her thoughts about Ivy League schools would have been the same; she just would have come up with a different way to dissuade me from Harvard. She had her reasons to resist the Ivy League and promote Catholic colleges and was committed to her view. She was a nun, for God's sake. If she wasn't promoting Catholic colleges over nonsectarian schools, who would be? I had my reasons, too, though, and was equally committed to my view. To quote an expression that became part of my vernacular later on, "That's what makes a market." Two valid opinions based on different perspectives.

Harvard was a hands-down great decision for me. No real shocker, but I absolutely loved it there. It was everything I hoped it could be and more. During the first few days of freshman orientation in the fall of 1983 we had a number of speakers make presentations to our new class. I remember that September sitting in Harvard Yard listening to various professors and administrators. At seventeen, I was taking it all in like a sponge, nervous and excited but still trying to listen. And even with the distractions of a new place, new people, new freedom, some of it penetrated. The dean of faculty, Henry Rosovsky, said something that always stuck with me. He said something like: "If you leave here when you graduate in four years thinking you actually know less than what you think you know right now, we have done our job well as faculty." That really sums up my experience at Harvard perfectly. As much as I studied hard and learned a tremendous amount in my four years, the bigger part of it was an eye-opener; a mind-opener to a whole wide world of people and ideas that I never knew existed. Even going home for my first Thanksgiving to my parents' house in Queens, just two months in, I felt like I was a drastically different person. Not because anything about my personality had changed, but because of what I had seen and heard and discovered. My universe had expanded a hundredfold. The world was a much bigger place than I'd ever imagined. There was more to know than I had conceded, and I now had less certitude.

Despite the fanfare and the significance of those first few days at Harvard, if you saw how I showed up that first day of college you would die laughing. Before you judge my fashion and hairstyle choices too quickly, remember it was the eighties. And I was from Queens. Even if I wasn't exactly a *Saturday Night Fever* character like some friends of mine from high school, it was a fine line. I thought I had picked the perfect outfit for that first day. I really chose it thoughtfully and carefully ahead of time. A matching gray sweatshirt miniskirt and top that had the neckline cut out à la *Flashdance*. To complement the look, I had some type of Madonna-ish hair tie, like a *Holiday* video-style thing. To complete the picture, I had recently permed my hair because no one wore straight hair anymore. The bigger the better. I would fit right in. I was always big on fashion and this was what passed for fashionable in my world. Harvard was a different galaxy altogether. Long, straight hair ruled the day.

If only the culture clash had started and stopped with the clothes. I also showed up with a thirteen-inch black and white television. Television was an important part of my life. Growing up, the televisions in our house were turned on 24-7. Literally, a bluish glow emanated from our home in Douglaston, Queens, if you drove by in the middle of the night. And I didn't exactly have high-class taste in television. Asked in one college interview what my favorite TV show was, I unabashedly said *Dynasty*, the great nighttime soap opera of the eighties. How could it not have been? It was so good. I felt no need to fake it and say *Nova* or *Masterpiece Theatre*. I loved to read and spent most of my free time reading classic literature, but my television tastes were decidedly lowbrow. But at Harvard in the early 1980s, hardly anyone showed up with televisions. Not to say Harvard students never watched TV, but I don't think they viewed it as a bare necessity like I did. Strike number two.

And then to top it all off, the *pièce de résistance*. I had insisted on bringing one of my most prized possessions: my Conair makeup mirror. I shared my dorm room with four other girls, and the mirror sat perfectly in the center of my desk. It was the mirror that gave you a day, night, and office light option. I remember the office light being some terrible greenish light, which luckily at that point didn't get used. I wasn't embarrassed. It seems now like I should have been, but I am happy to say I was not. I am proud of that. That was me. That was where I was from. It all worked in context, I just needed to make some adjustments, which I ended up doing over those first few months. I didn't reinvent myself in a fundamental way. Just some small changes of a more superficial nature. I started shopping for clothes at vintage stores in Harvard Square. The television never got turned on other than when I was trying to fall asleep at night. I don't remember for sure what happened to the makeup mirror, but it didn't come home with me that summer. I wish I could say the same of the perm, which took much longer to die its natural death.

I was fitting in at Harvard in a manageable and pretty small way. We're always making these adjustments, sensitive calibration to the environment around us, fine-tuning ourselves to belong without completely letting go of ourselves. Many years later when I became CFO of Lehman Brothers, I didn't know where the line was between small adjustments and more fundamental change as well as I did when I was seventeen. I wasn't as grounded later on, or as certain about who I was. You would think you would get better at that over time, not worse, wouldn't you? Know yourself better over time and be more confident in the "who" that you are. Well, from where I sit, that type of progress wasn't a given. I always assumed I knew myself better over the years, but really I think that just made it harder for other people to give me advice on my lifestyle. But in 1983, even with all my naïveté about life, I think I was doing just fine.

That first year of college challenged my prior notions of many things in my life, including the newly developed path I had laid out for myself. Of course I had a plan for post-college even before I started because it seemed important to know what you want to do with your life. My plan was to take premed courses, go to medical school right after college, and then ultimately practice medicine in the field of preventive medicine. Pretty specific, huh? How does a seventeen-year-old have this specific a plan? Probably because it wasn't really a plan I'd developed on my own. The plan had been conceived with my mother's help. There is nothing wrong with parents helping guide their children toward a goal that they deem worthy and good for them, but I was one of those kids who adopted it hook, line, and sinker. I liked chemistry, biology, and calculus. Why wouldn't I like being a doctor?

I took a full year of chemistry and calculus freshman year, which was in line with a premed agenda. For what it's worth, I got A's in those classes and enjoyed them, so things were going smoothly according to plan. When we retuned sophomore year we were expected to declare our majors that fall semester, which is earlier than in other schools. I was forced to examine, maybe for the first time, whether I really wanted to major in biology or something else to push me more definitively toward medical school. And I decided I didn't. It's hard to say what really made me think that I wanted to head in a different direction, but medicine just somehow didn't seem to appeal to me anymore. I had been exposed to so many things since I'd originally developed this plan that it felt outdated. It belonged to the old me, who was provincial, knew very little of life's possibilities. Changing the plan seemed like an evolution, and in line with what Henry Rosovsky had told us at freshman orientation. I was more aware of what I didn't know than ever before. How could I be locked into a vision of my life and career when I had just started?

Also—this sounds crazy given the career track I settled on—it occurred to me at the time that in some way the whole medical school path would also make having a family a real challenge. It would mean realistically starting to have children very late. I assumed it would be hard to start a family until you finished four years of medical school, an internship, and residency. I would be at least thirty before I believed it was practical to start having children.

Marriage and children were on my brain for the first time in my life because I'd met Chris at Harvard, my first serious boyfriend. For the first two years of college, I thought I was really in love, and a permanent relationship and kids were things I wanted, at least at that moment. It's ironic that at eighteen I was establishing old-fashioned, time-tested priorities that I ended up dismissing later on, the opposite of the many teens who reject the establishment and then gravitate toward it later in life. Of course, moving away from these priorities as time passed wasn't any kind of dramatic renunciation, mind you. Rather, my goals eroded from a slow attrition that comes from making a million little decisions that are inconsistent with the desired outcome. Now thirty years later, I have returned to these early priorities that got lost along the way. I think it helps to know what it looks like when you lose focus on what matters. Because it is subtle. And it is important to know that making my career the center of my universe was far from where I started.

After deciding against medicine, I moved on to become an American history major and it all seemed to work out at first. I went home for Thanksgiving sophomore year and updated my parents that I was dropping premed and majoring in history. The news went over like a lead balloon. My father tended to be less vocal, but my mother made it clear she hated the idea. How could I be dropping premed? I wasn't going to be a doctor? And as the history major piece sunk in, she said, "What are you going to do with history? Be a history professor? You are not going to like living on a college campus for your career."

It was as if I'd said I was going to drop out of school. She was really upset for at least an hour. I was shell-shocked. I hadn't expected her to be thrilled because she was such a fundamental part of developing the medical school idea, but to infer that I wouldn't achieve worldly success because I was a history major at Harvard with a 4.0 seemed a little crazy. In fairness to my mother, I think what bothered her most was that I'd made the decision on my own without even consulting her. That was new and unpleasant territory. We had a very close relationship, and my changing "our plan" unilaterally must have felt like a betrayal.

Switching majors was an important part of my growing up, because I started to think for myself about who I was and what I wanted.

While we argued, I don't think I even mentioned my worries about the ability to have a family and children, and I don't think it would have changed anything if I had. I just said that my interests had developed differently and I wanted to make a change.

I did become a history major even after the drama with my mother, but I didn't understand her reaction until much later on. Now it makes complete sense to me. As an adult, I now know how hard it is for parents to let their children become adults. I see my husband struggle with it constantly: wanting his children to be mature and self-sufficient but struggling with the sadness that comes from them not needing him in the same way they always have.

Though the drama with my mother was difficult, I'm proud to say that I was making pretty good decisions that matched my priorities. I had no idea what my career path would be with an American history major, but I loved history and I left the rest to hard work and chance. I had faith that things would work out even without a playbook.

As the next year of college went by, I hadn't really developed a better idea of precisely what I wanted to do when I graduated, but as I started the fall of senior year, one idea started to take hold. That summer I had spent six weeks at a graduate program in literature at Oxford. I had traveled with my parents to Europe for the first time about nine months prior and had managed side trips from London to both Cambridge and Oxford. After seeing those two great universities, I was awestruck. I was hell-bent on figuring out how to spend some time in one of those two places. I put effort into finding a program at Oxford that was run by Oxford faculty, not one of the American college programs. Luckily, the Oxford-run program was the least expensive and I made it through the selection process. That summer I met great people, including Elizabeth, a classmate from

Harvard whom I hadn't really know well from school before that summer. At the end of the program, a number of the American students were traveling for a few weeks and I begged my parents to let me join them on a shoestring budget. So I stretched a tiny budget over about two weeks in France and Italy, leading to a number of funny experiences and a bit of a life lesson.

Near the end of the second week, we traveled back from Milan to Paris on an overnight train. I remember my group of friends sleeping on the floor of the train at the far end of a car next to the door. At one point, the Italian police—the *carabinieri*—came by and gave us a hard time for sleeping there. They carried some kind of machine guns and didn't exactly have a soft approach. It was a little bit of an eye-opener, and it occurred to me for the first time that maybe I should pursue a career after school where I could make a little money. Make a good enough living that I could go to Europe and take a train and have a nice seat, for example. I wasn't thinking a lot of money, mind you, but at least enough money to live comfortably.

I got back a few weeks later to start the fall of senior year of college and applied to a handful of law schools. Talk about somewhat mundane experiences making a significant impact on big life decisions. I was behind in the whole law school application process at that point, so I had to plan to take the LSATs in December and figure out what city I might want to live in for the next three years. And, of course, most importantly, I had to get my parents to agree to fund law school. It helped to be the youngest in my family, which meant my parents had no more college tuition bills looming. I hoped maybe they could tolerate a few more years of financial stress than they'd expected, and they graciously did. My parents, Tom and Eileen Callan, always gave me everything I needed through these growing up years and that was a key ingredient of my success. They allowed me to stay focused on my goals without worrying about the circumstances necessary to achieve them. I can fully appreciate and be grateful for that good fortune as an adult.

I told myself for a year that I was applying to law school because it would be a great starting point for learning how to think logically and thoughtfully. How could that not be useful for whatever I did after? I wasn't necessarily going to practice law, I just wanted a great education. It was a noble intellectual concept, and probably not one my parents would have been a fan of if I had articulated it clearly at the time. It was a way to convince myself I had not made a permanent decision about my life, because I didn't really feel prepared to do that. If I could look at law as three years of schooling rather than a thirty-year career, it would be easier to swallow. That worked for me. I am always amazed by others who have a big goal and pursue it tirelessly over many years. I'm not sure how many twenty-year-olds wake up and say, "I want to be a CEO someday." They must exist, but I was not one of them. That was not in my DNA.

Is it disappointing that I didn't have some master plan to get a legal education and then ply my talents on Wall Street? To train myself in critical thinking through the practice of law and then apply that discipline to the financial markets? That what really happened was I applied to law school because I'd slept on a dirty floor of a train and been hassled by the police? The irony is that later in my career I would meet young women at the college level and they would tell me they were thinking about pursuing my path: going to law school, practicing law for a few years, and then going to Wall Street to nail down their success. Funny, huh? My brilliant plan. I would tell them very simply that if they wanted to work on Wall Street, go to Wall Street now.

Why circle around in a different direction first? It is comforting to think that formulas exist, and it's not so random, but for me it was pretty random. If I had relied on a blueprint rather than life experiences, I would have ended up in preventive medicine.

Once I finished law school, I inevitably ended up practicing law. Environments create their own momentum for better or worse, and almost as soon as I got to NYU Law School in the fall of 1987, I was carried on the wave breaking at the shores of the large, New York corporate law firms. My theoretical pursuit of a legally educated mind led to a practical end. And that was okay. Sometimes the original motivation mutates, but the outcome is still good. But at twenty-four years old, as I accepted an offer to work at one of those large firms, I was in a real work environment for the first time in a serious way. It would be the beginning of almost a twenty-year period where I became singularly devoted to my career. I had no clue at twenty-four that I was headed that way. I was just trying to make my way in the world, be self-sufficient, feel accomplished and productive. Nothing unusual or unconventional. It is hard to say that's how it turned out, though.

CHAPTER THREE

Unforgivable Sins

I ALWAYS BELIEVED my work life and personal life needed to be kept very separate. That was my idea of what it meant to be professional. To me, when I was in my mid-twenties, being professional somehow meant presenting yourself as some disembodied brain. Pure intellectual capacity. I thought gender should be taken out of the equation as much as possible. There is nothing wrong with maintaining a certain decorum in the work environment, but I think—like a lot of things—I took it a little too far. In my first job as a lawyer, I don't think I ever brought my true self to work, and ultimately that was part of the dissatisfaction that after five years of practicing law ultimately led me in a new direction.

So what did I look like as a "professional"? It's a little hard to describe, but I generally didn't talk about life outside of work with my colleagues. I did have a few good friends I worked with who were in the same class of law associates that started at the New York firm Simpson Thacher & Bartlett in 1990. I would share bigger life events with them, but I really limited it to that group. Granted, the environment was significantly more formal than the one I came to revel in on

Wall Street. At Simpson Thacher, like most large law firms, there was a clearly defined hierarchy with no shortcuts. You started out of law school as an associate and the earliest you could be considered for partner was after seven years. Partnership, at least at that time in the early 1990s, was like getting tenure as a professor at a university. Once you were a partner, you were a partner for good. So there was a great divide between the two basic roles of associates and partners. With the sixty or so associates who started with me at the firm, maybe six or seven would ultimately end up as partners. And at that time, every associate in your class got paid the same amount of money, for better or worse. It was all about the carrot of partnership down the road. The better you were at the job, the more in demand you were, and the longer hours you worked. Doing your job well was an invitation to work harder for the same pay. A real catch-22. The rewards of the firm were all about playing for the future and the system was what it was.

There was something appealing about the whole setup to me, even though I was one of the better associates who worked more hours. I liked the idea that there were no shortcuts. I was always willing to work hard for a reward down the road, and I liked the idea that if I put in the work, there was a lot of consistency and certainty to it. To adjust to this system, I created a set of rules for myself. I would go in every day (which usually meant six days a week at least), give it my all mentally, and then go home and live my life. It was a construct that was bound to be unfulfilling, or at a minimum, unrealistic over the long run. But at least at this point I wasn't too extreme; there *was* room to live my life, even though work was very important to me.

I had only been at Simpson Thacher for a couple of years when I went back to my five-year college reunion at Harvard. Given that I had loved Harvard and almost everything about my four years there, the fifth reunion turned out to be a good example of what I most appreciated. It was the first time I saw all my friends from college in one place after graduation, and they had all done very cool things. My friend Margy had spent time in the Peace Corps in Africa for several years, my friend Greg had attended Berklee School of Music in Boston and then moved to Spain to play in a band, and so on. Of course there was a core group that had moved to New York and were working at Goldman and other Wall Street firms, but even that seemed pretty glamorous. When asked what I was doing, I was almost embarrassed. I had to say, "I am a corporate tax lawyer," because that was the naked truth, but somehow it seemed terribly unflattering. There's no way to beat around the bush with that one. It wasn't sexy or cool, nor was it a whole host of other good adjectives that were seemingly apt for everyone else's lives. I had never tried to be too cool, but I was still self-conscious.

Was this who I was meant to be? The fulfillment of my childhood dreams? I certainly didn't grow up thinking I wanted to be a tax lawyer. Does anyone, really? I hope not. That's not a knock on tax lawyers, but just an honest statement of how we like to see ourselves. In third grade, I'd written an essay about how I wanted to be an astronomer. Now I started to worry about an obituary that would read "practiced tax law for fifty years."

But, though I didn't like to think of myself as a tax lawyer, the reality was that I liked the job itself. I genuinely liked it. And, most importantly, it suited my temperament and my intellect. Being a corporate tax lawyer was the sum of many decisions I'd made in my early twenties during the process of figuring out who I was and what drove me. In no way did it jive with how I imagined myself, but that was okay. A good friend at Lehman, Greg, later used to tease me that I was the guy with the green eyeshade in the back room peering fastidiously over the books, and I guess I was. But it worked for me at the time even if it didn't match up with the picture in my head.

There certainly was an advantage to being a tax lawyer, rather than a litigation or corporate lawyer, because I tended to consult on lots of deals and projects, but not to be at the center of any one of them. That decision saved me because I suspect I would have let things get out of whack much sooner had I been the main point person to clients in those early years of practicing law. That's part of why I chose tax practice during the initial six months of my first year working, figuring that having a secondary role in most cases would mean I was able to have a little better control of my life. Equally important to me was that for young tax lawyers the work was high quality and intellectual from the beginning. There was very little of the grunt work that existed in spades in the corporate and litigation practices. There was a lot of workload consistency, and I was much less subject to the vagaries and volatility of one particular deal's life cycle. Of course, if the good news was more consistent workweeks, the bad news was that they tended to be reliably long and hard.

Rob, my boyfriend at the time, used to tease me about how much I liked work. We'd been dating since my second year of law school at NYU, but he was a year ahead of me so he had already been working for a year at another large New York law firm, Skadden Arps, by the time I started at Simpson Thacher. Rob was over the initial fun you have when you realize you have your first serious job. He was working long hours each week and the bloom was off the rose. I was in first flush with the job and thought everything about it was great, and I didn't appreciate what I'd labeled at the time as his cynicism. It really created some issues in our relationship. The book *Learned Optimism* was relatively new then. I remember him reading it, in part because I had complained that he couldn't see how good everything was, including our jobs. He was reading it for me. For us. Looking back, I'm guessing Rob really didn't have a problem with me liking my job. He had a problem with me not giving him enough attention. He didn't want to talk about work all the time like I did. He didn't want me to go out after work with my work friends after I'd spent all day with them. The more he tried different methods to get my attention, the harder I fought it.

It only took working two years before we broke up. He really was a great person, but I had decided he was trying to control me, which was an unforgivable sin in my book. All Rob really wanted was to have more of me. The dirty secret was that my pledge to separate my work and personal life was, in actuality, starting to mean not letting my personal life interfere with work. And, even worse, that led to letting work control my personal life. I guess it was just more acceptable for me to blame him for trying to control me rather than admit I was losing myself to my job. Control is one of my go-to excuses in relationships. Feeling like my partner is trying to control me is the unpardonable offense. Really, it was just a convenient way for me to justify doing whatever the hell it is I wanted to do without regard to the other person. I still fight this instinct. When my husband, Anthony, wants a lot from me, my time, attention, and energy, he reminds me that is not a crime. Not a flaw. Not a fundamental disconnect. I should be thrilled he finds me so compelling. But when I'm angry, I still go there. Luckily I am not angry often and I can see the pattern in my behavior rationally to combat the urge to fight what is good for me.

After Rob, there was still work, where I was happy. I thought my life outside of work would take care of itself. Work required my care and focus. I still wasn't too crazy yet, though. I was a strong performer at Simpson Thacher. I was extremely disciplined, hardworking, and a good problem solver. I also understood that in the end we were in a client service business and getting things right for the client was of paramount importance.

In these early days I started to create my own personal process for how to be effective in my job. I really thrived working on a multitude of projects and with many clients. Most of the clients I worked with were Wall Street firms, and Lehman Brothers was the one firm I spent the most time with. We were Lehman's law firm in many areas of the tax practice. A substantial part of the tax advice we gave Lehman related to the development of new financial products. For me, this was intriguing. I had never imagined the creativity that would be involved in the world of finance, having had so little exposure up to that point. I was an American history major after all, though I am not sure if I had been an economics major I would have been more enlightened. Harvard had no business-related majors like finance. Once I started to learn about the panoply of financial products, however, I expressed my interest and ran with it. I analyzed and summarized every new product development across the capital markets for the benefit of the tax and corporate groups at Simpson, studying the prospectuses and writing up summaries of the significant terms and consequences. Synthesizing these developments in understandable ways was of high value to the firm, and I thought it was cool. I was pretty quickly the new products point person in our tax group. In retrospect, it wasn't some unique DNA coding I had for understanding new products, I think I was just ready to dive into something. It could have been a lot of different things, but I had a great desire to get smart about something and differentiate myself quickly. My friend Nancy from Lehman would later say that "our employers love us for our neuroses." I always knew exactly what she meant. I was always looking for self-worth at work, where it was much less complicated to find than in real life. I got off to a quick start on that one.

I have to mention, very importantly, that in this whole area of new products I worked with a partner, Dickson Brown, who was a great teacher and mentor to me. Dickson had been managing the Wall Street relationships at Simpson Thacher for the taxation of capital instruments and new products for several years. From the first time I worked with him on a project, we clicked, which was far from a given because there were several associates who were afraid of him. They thought he was tough and critical. He was certainly demanding, but he also gave the associates who worked for him a lot of responsibility, and I loved that. Your role was meaningful even though you were only a few months out of law school. You got to speak as the expert on client conference calls about the research you'd done on an issue. Don't get me wrong. If you messed up, it wasn't good, but he trusted you. He was relying on you. There was little to no margin for error. But if you were thoughtful, thorough, and diligent, he let you run with things.

So, lucky me, really. I worked with Dickson early on at Simpson Thacher, and for the next five years I worked with him significantly more than any other partner in the tax department or at the firm. After a year or so, the counterparts at Lehman would call me directly when they had questions, which made Dickson happy. He viewed my role as complementary to his and never found me threatening. After I left Simpson Thacher to work for Lehman and worked with Dickson from the other side as the client, I saw him do this with a few other associates over the years. He was a very smart and talented tax lawyer, but he really was a fantastic developer of talent. That was a unique attribute in a large New York law firm where so much focus at the partner level was on the partner's own production and client relationships. Luckily, I don't have to figure out if I would have been as successful anyway without Dickson's support early in my career. But I do know that for my part I didn't let myself be scared off by his reputation, and I ran with the opportunity he gave me. My close friends at work used to tease me that I was Dickson's "favorite." Work can be no different than high school sometimes. But if I really was his favorite, I earned it. I rose to the occasion. We did work together for years after I went to Lehman because I still needed outside tax advice on projects, and our relationship didn't end when I left Wall Street. In fact, every year on my birthday he still sends me an e-mail. It's funny that he still remembers, but I shouldn't be surprised.

In certain respects, things were going well for several years at Simpson Thacher. Outside of work, things kept moving too. Soon after Rob and I broke up, I met another very nice guy, Austin, who was a friend of my sister's from her job. I never seemed to have a problem meeting people and starting relationships. I usually jumped in quickly and completely. It was in the actual follow-through that I stumbled. Ironically, Austin worked at Lehman and had been there since graduating from college four years prior, but I had never dealt with him in my Simpson Thacher work with Lehman. We started dating and became serious pretty quickly. I probably should have taken some time before I got involved in another relationship because I never reflected properly on why Rob and I hadn't worked out. I was twenty-six years old, however, so maybe I shouldn't have been sur-

prised. I had made up my mind that I blamed our crumbling relationship on Rob's wish to dictate what I did, and the direction of my life.
As the modern career woman, I needed self-determination and free
will. In a relationship, we were supposed to be equals, which to me
meant that I got to live by my rules and agenda. Correspondingly he
could live by his, though I am not sure I really believed that part. Live
and let live. No compromises. At least no real ones. He wasn't willing
to meet those terms, so the relationship was over. Even after four years
of Rob and I being together in a serious way, I was able to adjust
without him just fine.

Over the next few years, Austin and I dated, got engaged, and
bought an apartment together. All the while, I chugged along at work,
working hard but not obsessively like I would later on.

If I learned anything about having success in your career, it is that
the extreme positive reinforcement you get for doing well at work is
such a huge motivator. There is a very tangible and real sense of accomplishment from clients and colleagues that you don't get in such
an obvious way in your real life. The harder the work, the more you
achieve, the more kudos you get. In the rest of your life, it can be
much harder to quantify success. I didn't know how common that line
of thinking is until recently. An article published in the *New York
Times* in 2014 discussed a Penn State study that found that people's
stress levels are actually lower at work than at home. To quote the article, "The finding suggests that for many people, the workplace is a
sort of haven away from life's daily problems" (*NYT,* May 22, 2014,
"Is Work Your Happy Place?"). Work offers a less messy reality. We
feel more clearly appreciated and valued because the guideposts are
more obvious, at least enough of the time. That tells me now that we
don't do a good enough job letting the people we love know what they

mean to us. That they are cherished. Home should be the haven, if we treat each other properly. But for years, work was the happier place for me. At the firm, and to an even greater extent at Lehman, this feeling was an addiction for me. I was driven by those highs that I felt I experienced uniquely at work. But unlike with a drug addiction, the more extreme I was, the more positive the feedback.

It wasn't just me. Among the law associates at Simpson Thacher that I worked with, I remember it being a badge of honor for whoever had worked the most hours in any given year. Did you work three thousand hours this year or maybe even thirty-two hundred? We all respected that. It seems crazy now. Why did we respect it? That's over sixty hours every single week of the year. No vacation. That's terrible, but it was universally admired. At this point in my career, I hadn't reached that point. I worked a lot but I didn't work three thousand hours a year. But the culture was there for extremism, and even if I didn't opt in 100 percent, I didn't have a problem with it. In fact, I respected it. I understood it.

About three years into my relationship with Austin things started to go off the rails a bit. It wasn't an uncommon pattern—although all my relationships tended to be long, four to five years, they never made it much longer. Austin and I were engaged but things started deteriorating three to four months before the wedding we'd planned for September 1995. It's hard for me to pinpoint exactly what took us in the wrong direction, but I certainly managed to get along just fine at work while this was happening. No one at my office knew a thing. That's not something I'm proud of now, but I admired my own determination at the time. The way I look at things, my *weltanschauung*, had no small role I am sure in where things ended up with Austin and me. For some reason one story comes to mind every time I think about Austin and our relationship. How we had such a great connection that didn't stick.

One night in late 1994, Austin and I walked to the local pizzeria for a bite to eat. We strolled from the apartment we had bought together on East End Avenue. It was a first for both of us to own a home. It was a great time for us, new homeowners, newly engaged, both with good jobs living in Manhattan. We had fun with each other and had no real worries in life in our late twenties. We were happy, or at least I am sure we came across as happy. We should have been. We sat in the pizzeria and talked about life as usual. We talked about another couple we were friends with who were having some troubles in their relationship. They were originally friends of Austin's and the two of them had always seemed like a personality mismatch to me. We debated whether they were out of sync, whether their qualities didn't match up. And then something occurred to me and I asked him, "Well, if someone asked you what is the one thing you like about me the most, what would you say?" I waited and anticipated in my head his answer. We had been together a few years at that point and I thought I knew what his answer would be. He replied quickly, without any hesitation, "How pretty you are."

He stopped me dead in my tracks. I was flabbergasted. What? How pretty I was? That was my most important attribute? I was offended and overwhelmed. I am off base, right, for being offended? Yes, I was wrong. Who doesn't want their boyfriend or husband to tell you how pretty he thinks you are? But in my warped mind, there was nothing unique about being pretty. There were lots of pretty girls. And I assumed any "pretty" I had would go away as I got older. Why would this be a reason to stay together over the long run? Being pretty was not part of the way I saw myself. I was smart, damn it. That was what differentiated me from other girls. I was smart and successful. If he didn't see that as the most important thing about me, then did he really know who I was?

Poor Austin. He didn't deserve such a complicated reaction. I should have just said, "Thank you, sweetheart." Was it so bad to be pretty or have Austin think I was pretty? Was it demeaning? Did it have to undermine whatever other qualities I had? Today I am almost at the other end of the spectrum. My husband, Anthony, tells me every day how beautiful he thinks I am, and nothing means more to me. When he looks at me, he sees everything about me embodied in my physical form. Beauty is a quality that exists only in reference to another person. I can be smart in a vacuum. Intelligent is absolute, not relative. But if I am beautiful, it's because someone else thinks that about me. It is Anthony's perspective that matters to me. Any other qualities that I have don't suffer as a result, but rather are part of that opinion. You are beautiful means I love you. I love who you are. I love what I see when I look at you. I couldn't live without that now.

But with Austin, I had no such enlightenment. Instead of making me feel good, it troubled me. I allowed it to get into my head that he didn't really get the true me. He loved me for the wrong reasons. Once that idea was in my head, I don't think I ever let it out again. So when we hit a bad patch in our relationship the following year I was quick to be convinced that our relationship had failed. Maybe I would not have let things go so easily or would have tried harder to make it work if we hadn't had that conversation. It was an innocent comment over pizza, but I didn't forget it. I still don't, though now for different reasons than at that time.

There was so much more to it than that, of course. There always is. I don't think I made Austin feel good about himself. I think he had an image of who he wanted to be and he thought he could be that with me. Maybe he wanted to be someone more sophisticated, worldly, and successful than who he was in his mid- to late twenties, and I think he saw me as a great partner for that idealized version of himself. It always seemed like he was trying a little too hard, but I didn't do anything to make it better. I should have helped him feel good about who he was at the time. I didn't encourage him to change; I just didn't do anything, so he strived to be different. And I let him strive. Eventually, I think he felt he was failing me and himself. I know from subsequent experiences, it is almost impossible to be around someone long-term if you think you are failing them. It doesn't make you happy. And as time passed, Austin wasn't happy.

By this summer of 1995, Austin moved out and the engagement was over. Certainly a big life change, but I was still getting up every morning and going to work as usual. Something had fundamentally changed, though. I decided I should try to change work in addition to changing my personal life. Maybe, like my relationship with Austin, work was not everything I thought it was, either. Everything needed to be scrutinized. Now, logically, when you go through a big change in part of your life, it helps to keep the rest stable. Maybe when you make one big decision it's not so wise to make other big ones at the same time. You might actually make an emotional decision, not a rational one. Although I prided myself on not being emotional, the decision I made in 1995 to leave Simpson Thacher and my career practicing law to go to work at Lehman Brothers was an emotional one. I feel very certain that I never would have even considered a career change if Austin and I had not broken up. There would have been no overwhelming desire for change.

None of this means leaving the law and going to work on Wall Street was a bad decision. It ended up being a good decision, motivated in part by very reasonable considerations. By five years into my legal career, what had been appealing at the outset had really now become a fatal flaw. I wanted to be more relevant to my clients, more at the center of things. I didn't love being a consultant. I wanted to have a significant, critical role. As a tax lawyer that just wasn't going to happen. Also, after those years of exposure to Wall Street from the outside looking in, I started to notice something that really resonated with me. The people I worked with at the Wall Street firms like Lehman, Swiss Bank, and Goldman were passionate about their jobs. They appeared to have great enthusiasm and excitement. No one was going through the motions. On the other hand, I had always sensed a certain apathy in the world of big law firms. I certainly had many talented and smart colleagues, but several talked rather wistfully about what else they could be doing with their lives if they weren't practicing law. It was the "lawyer's malaise" as I called it. In the mid-1990s, being a corporate lawyer at a big New York firm brought you right to the fringe of the circle of excitement around deal making and the capital markets. But you were always just shy of the mark, like somebody standing at the velvet ropes at a club hoping to get let in. At least that's how it felt to me. And I decided I wanted in.

CHAPTER FOUR

No Rearview Mirror

WHEN I DECIDED at twenty-eight years old that I needed a career change, I also decided that I wanted to go work at Lehman. Nowhere else. In my role at Simpson Thacher I had been working with the new products and capital markets groups at Lehman virtually every day for years, and it mattered to me more than anything that I knew the team of people at the firm well. It never occurred to me to talk to a headhunter or interview at any other Wall Street firm. The Lehman team seemed to love being there and that meant a lot in my book. Although at points in its history Lehman had been an independent firm, in 1984 it had been acquired by American Express. The marriage didn't last long, and in 1994 Lehman was spun off as an independent firm again. When I was considering my move to Lehman only a year later in 1995, the recent spin-off created challenges as Lehman forged ahead as a small investment bank among larger, established players. None of this potentially concerning context factored into my decision. The matter at hand was to figure out how to get a job there.

In the early summer of 1995, I called my client Neil, who ran the preferred capital raising group at Lehman. After some project small talk, I gathered my courage for the question, "Hey, Neil, on a different note, do you think someone like me could work on Wall Street?" I said it as a friend seeking advice because I really thought he could give me honest feedback after our working together for years. He knew my skills and personality, which was ideal, but still made me nervous, since his answer would be an experienced and honest assessment. He wouldn't BS me. If he said no, I didn't really have a game plan, but I had quickly come to a place where I desperately wanted change, and I couldn't put off pursuing it any longer.

"When can you get down here to interview?" he said enthusiastically. "We could never go after you because it's like poaching. You are our lawyer. It's out of bounds. But, since you came to me, we are okay. I just need to talk to some people." And there it was. We were off to the races. Between early summer and when I officially received an offer in mid-September of 1995, I must have had interviews with twenty or more people at Lehman. It seemed like a lot, since I knew so many people there already, and I certainly didn't have a lot of free time to interview. The day of our annual summer outing at Simpson Thacher that August, I managed to bow out of it and spent the entire day at Lehman. I felt guilty about it at the time, but it seemed like the most efficient strategy to avoid dropping the ball on any of my Simpson Thacher projects.

A few people I interviewed with at Lehman were a little mystified about how a corporate tax lawyer would fit in as a capital markets banker. I had to insist that I had no intention to go work in the legal department at Lehman Brothers. I wanted a new career path. I wanted to be an investment banker.

I sat in one interview with a gentleman named John who worked in a department called Central Funding. As was the case with a lot of people I was interviewing with, I didn't have a clue as to what his group did or how he related to the job I might have there. In all honesty, I don't think I really understood what my job at Lehman was going to be. In hindsight it seems like I was being a little reckless. Or maybe I was just relying on good instincts. Depends on how you want to spin it. In any event, I think John thought my credentials were pretty unorthodox. He seemed confused by me. "So what deals would you bring with you?" he asked hopefully. He didn't get it. I didn't have any deals. I was a lawyer. No one awarded you deals as a lawyer, at least not the kind he was talking about. I somehow talked him past that concept. I tried to clarify my qualifications. "Well, then, what new product structures do you have?" he asked a little later, as if I had a bag of tricks. I was picturing Santa Claus in my head walking around with a big bag of toys. In John's defense, later I came to know people on Wall Street that did peddle their bag of tricks, leveraging product ideas to get buy-in. I didn't have anything like that. So somehow we got through the interview, which led to several more, but it was a bit of an experiment on all sides.

We were all taking a leap of faith. Except Neil, who was completely confident that it would work out, and that gave me the courage of my convictions. I give him all the credit in the world for that. Prior to my resignation from Simpson Thacher I'd imagined there would be another small tide that I might be fighting: my parents. My dad had started his working life as a police officer in New York City like his father before him. But a few years into the job, he applied for and won an NYPD scholarship to attend Brooklyn Law School. When he completed law school after four years of night classes, he made the transition from beat cop to the NYPD Legal Division. By the time that I was contemplating leaving the field of law, my dad, having retired from the NYPD in the mid-1980s after putting in his twenty years of service, had had his own legal practice for several years. My mother was working in commercial real estate for a title insurance company after having been a stay-at-home mom until I left for college. In this new life, she spent her days surrounded by real estate lawyers at large Manhattan law firms. Both of them viewed working at an elite law firm like Simpson Thacher & Bartlett as a big accomplishment, which it was of course. They didn't know too much about Wall Street and I suspect didn't view it as matching the professionalism, prestige, and dignity of a white-shoe law firm. And to add insult to injury, I was only a few years from making partner. Why would I give that up for something I knew nothing about?

That line of reasoning would have been fair, but luckily they didn't make a big deal out of it. I got the sense that they were uncomfortable and confused as to why I would want to jump into those unknown waters. I needed a life change. A change I wasn't making in my personal life with my relationships. I let that beat continue in its same rhythm. At the time I wouldn't have seen it this way, but now I think I probably wanted a more exciting work environment to make up for boredom with my personal life.

Resigning was no easy task. The one and only time I was in the head of Simpson Thacher's office during the five years that I worked there was in mid-September of 1995 to resign. That was the way you were supposed to do it. Dick Beattie was the head of the firm and had a reputation as a tough, no-nonsense ex-marine. Although we may have met before that day, we were not familiar with each other. But based on what he knew about me, his goal was to talk me out of leaving. Dick Beattie is an imposing character and maybe not coincidentally shares certain positive characteristics with Dick Fuld, who was the CEO of Lehman Brothers. To put it simply, it wasn't going to be easy to get out of his office with plans intact. "You know you'll make partner in a few years?" he opened. "You've been doing great and you have a future here," he continued. I felt like Charlie Brown when the teacher is talking. It was just noise. He spent a half hour with me and tried hard to convince me I was making a big mistake. I recognize that a half hour of his time was very valuable and I should have been flattered. I didn't waver.

As he started to close his argument he tried the most basic persuasive point, "You'll make more money if you stay here, you know." A dramatic pause followed, but that wasn't the right angle with me. It wasn't an illogical guess on his part, but money wasn't what motivated me. I really didn't care about the money as much as I wanted to thrive professionally. To be great at what I did and be recognized for it in an environment surrounded by other people like me. This conversation did not phase me because I was absolutely convinced I needed this big transformation in my life and it needed to happen now.

His final remark still makes me laugh to this day. He could see he was making no headway, so he cut his losses, switched gears, and tried to give me some advice. "You should at least interview at Goldman." And there it was. Lehman did much more business at the time with Simpson Thacher than Goldman had ever done, but there was still a Goldman mystique. In 1995, Lehman seemed like an odd choice to him for someone on the fast track like me. Lehman was a fledgling, independent company—albeit with a long history—and was having challenges. There was no changing my mind. Significant, dramatic change was the only option imaginable to me. After I broke off my engagement with Austin, my passion for work at Simpson had died on the vine.

Did I think changing my job would relieve the disappointment of not getting married as I'd planned? Was there really an issue with work, or was my personal life creating too much static for me to see clearly? I didn't know the true answers to those questions, but I knew in my gut the decision was right for me.

When you leave a law firm, they don't walk you out the door with security that same day with all your stuff in tow. There were so many projects I would have to hand off and things to teach the younger lawyers about what I'd been doing. I worked for six more weeks to make the transition smooth and fulfill what I thought were my obligations to people and a place that had been good to me. Lehman was restless to get me going, though, so I couldn't manage any time off. At least that's how I saw it, of course. It would have been a perfect time to take a break, but I didn't even think of it. I was chomping at the bit to get going in a new direction. I finally finished up at Simpson Thacher on a Friday afternoon and started at Lehman that following Monday morning, October 30, 1995. Dickson and some other colleagues threw me a farewell lunch and surprisingly I didn't feel too bad about leaving. I was looking forward as always. I never had much of a rearview mirror. I was ready to go.

I would be working for Neil at Lehman Brothers. During the long interview process, Neil had figured out how to create a spot for me in his group. It was an ideal situation: an exciting and new job with just enough familiarity with the people in the group to feel immediately like a part of a team. I never could have imagined where this job would lead me.

Since I hadn't spent a lot of time thinking about the practical specifics of my job at Lehman, it was easy for it to beat expectations. But that understates how much I loved it, right from the very beginning.

All the energy and enthusiasm that surrounded me filled the void that had existed after Austin and I broke up. The period for a few years after I started at Lehman was the longest I went in my adult life without a serious relationship. That made it easy to let work fill in as many gaps as it could. Like the spray foam insulation they shoot into house framing, so that it can seep into every nook and cranny. I had no real distractions, and the more I let work dominate my life, the better I seemed to do at it.

Timing is everything, and it was for me when I landed at Lehman. The team I joined was responsible for developing and marketing certain types of preferred stock and securities. Not so coincidentally, these types of financial instruments had been under the scrutiny of the Internal Revenue Service at that point in time and the federal tax treatment was a focal point. In large part, this tax scrutiny was the reason I had been working so closely with the Lehman team prior to being hired. This tax contention allowed me to shine. In my first few years at Lehman, the main priority of our clients with respect to preferred securities was the tax classification. I was an expert. I was a tax lawyer, not another investment banker who needed to rely on the advice of counsel. I had complete credibility. There was no need for third-party witnesses.

Ironically, having a law degree versus a master's degree in business was not a negative, but a distinct and positive advantage. So what happened? Clients gravitated toward our Lehman team when it came to awarding this type of business. We had the unique knowledge and I was a critical part of the formula for that success. My confidence grew with my marketing skills. And while I rode the wave of technical expertise, I bought myself time to develop a working knowledge that I was lacking of how financial markets operated, not just the products themselves. After a couple of years, I came up the learning curve on market knowledge to match my product knowledge.

I was flying all over the country with my colleagues several days a week. visiting treasurers and chief financial officers of large corporations who wanted to listen to our advice. When I was in the office, we were executing transactions mandated to us by these clients. It was frenetic and I was exhilarated with the success. The business was soaring and within Lehman we were getting recognition as a center of excellence. Along the way, I managed to develop a reputation inside and outside of Lehman as a smart, technical banker and a savvy marketer. I loved it.

It's not as if there were no hiccups, but they were few and far between. I had only been working at Lehman a few months when I headed out on the road to the West Coast to see several bank clients with some colleagues. We were seeing six or seven clients in a few days. The basic concept of the presentations we were making would be the same, but each presentation book had to be tailored to a particular bank. It's always chaotic trying to get this many presentations done, and our group was carrying about seventy presentation books to the airport. One of our first few meetings was with Washington Mutual. It was one of the biggest thrifts in the country at the time in 1995 and a meaningful client of Lehman's. Well, lo and behold, there was a major screw-up. The entire presentation referred to the Federal Reserve as the regulator of Washington Mutual, when their regulator was the Office of Thrift Supervision. For those not familiar with finance, I should point out that it mattered a lot. It would be almost like referring to the NBA when talking to an NFL team. Not quite as bad, but not so far off. It would have mattered in any event, but particularly because what we were recommending for them to do was contingent on their regulator's approval. And, boy, did it look so careless, like we'd just slapped their name on a presentation for another client. Which was kind of what we'd done. We had a generic presentation where the names could just be subbed in and out. Just terrible.

Minutes after we were out the door from the Washington Mutual meeting, my colleague received an irate phone call from one of the Lehman fixed income salesmen in New York. He'd already heard from his counterpart at Washington Mutual about the meeting and our presentation. In those few minutes, he'd already stormed into his boss's office in New York to complain vociferously about what we'd done. Not exactly the way you want to make an impression on your new colleagues. It was so embarrassing, especially since I prided myself on attention to detail. I had definitely been a bit over my head with the whole road trip happening so soon after I started. It showed. I never got it together and reviewed all the presentations the way I should have, with a painstaking, page-by-page approach for each presentation. I was trying to juggle too many things at once before we left on the trip.

The sins committed on that road trip didn't end there. On the last day and the last client meeting we were in Salt Lake City meeting with Zion's Bank and we literally had the wrong bank's name on the cover of the presentation. Scrambling quickly, we had to pull all the cover pages off just before we walked into the conference room to sit down. It looked ridiculous not to have a cover page, but it was better than having the wrong name I suppose.

Luckily for us, the treasurer of Zion's Bank was a good guy and laughed it off. I haven't mentioned there were still incorrect references in other parts of the book, but they were not as glaring as the cover. But, Jesus, the wrong name? The recovery from the road trip was not easy. I didn't score any points for meticulous work product and I was appalled. I wasn't the only one who had worked on the presentations, but ultimately we were discussing my product ideas so I took accountability for it. A dubious debut. As a perfectionist, it pained me, but I had to bounce back, and quickly. Understand that we all make mistakes. Yes. All of us. Even me. Lesson learned. I understand that so well these days as I find I make a lot of mistakes constantly. Sometimes I think of it as being a novice at my new version of life, compared to being an expert at my old version. There is some truth to that, but even more so, I think I am more open to recognizing my mistakes, admitting to them, and trying to take something from them. As my second grade teacher Sister Christopher used to tell us, "If you can't learn from your mistakes, there's no sense in making them." As a child, I thought this logic was laughable and the saying stuck with me as more amusing then anything. As an adult, I know what she means.

With the success at work, normal, conventional life started to fade. A good example of how I'd started to immerse myself in my career at this point was reflected in a notice I received from Con Edison, my electric utility, in late 1996. The notice asked if I wanted my natural gas shut off in my apartment, since I hadn't used it for more than eighteen months. That means I'd never turned on my stove for all that time, not even to boil water. Some domestic life I had, huh? But things were going great at work and I thought I was happy. I mean, honestly, if I thought I was happy, I probably was, right?

I truly believe happiness is a choice. Anthony and I were having Chinese food recently and the fortune in his fortune cookie was "Happiness is not a reward, it's a consequence." What a great fortune, and something we both believe to our core. I was choosing to be happy, and I hadn't yet realized that I required more. I never looked back.

Success with clients quickly piled up when I got to Lehman. We were winning more business as a firm. My decision was more than validated.

I didn't spend any time thinking about being lonely, but I was lonely. With all the hubbub that took place at work, when I opened the door to my apartment at night in those first few years at Lehman, there was no one else at home. I was unprepared for not being in a relationship for that long. I had loved having a partner, someone to share my life with, even if I didn't always give that person the full attention they deserved. I would eat crazy meals because I couldn't be bothered with dinner. Frozen yogurt picked up on the way home was sometimes my most important meal of the day. I did crosswords to fill time at home, however limited it was, and voraciously plowed through books. It wasn't so bad that I had cats, but I did have two small dogs, which isn't much better. My relationship surrogates. Sounds like a bad Lifetime movie? Woman with huge career living this pathetic, little life after work. My version of leaning in to my career at this point in my life didn't look so glamorous on close examination, no matter how well I was doing at work.

Although these couple of years felt long, I did start dating someone seriously again in 1997. His name was Peter and he worked at Lehman. I know, I know! But where else was I supposed to meet someone who would understand my work-dominated lifestyle? Also, practically speaking, it's not like I got out that much.

And with all that was going well at work, the headhunters came knocking quickly. I wasn't used to being headhunted as a lawyer. It's probably common now, but wasn't at the time. You typically went to work at a law firm out of law school, made it through the seven or eight years as an associate, and if you were lucky and good enough to make partner, that was that. Lifelong tenure. I brought that way of thinking to Lehman. Switching careers had meant I'd had to switch firms, but now this was it. This is where I would stay. I didn't know about the temptations that came with high performance, the promise of the "big job" somewhere else. After less than two years at Lehman, I got a call from a headhunter that Credit Suisse was interested in hiring me to run their preferred securities business in capital markets. Basically, it was analogous to my boss Neil's job at Lehman. To my boyfriend, Peter, this was good news and par for the course for good people on Wall Street. He'd worked on the Street much longer than I had and the dynamic of other firms trying to woo you away was normal to him. I don't think he felt the emotion and loyalty that I ascribed to my job and its circumstances. His view was you worked to make money, so if you could make more somewhere else, then you should take advantage of the offer. His job wasn't the complete center of his existence. There was a reason they paid you to do the work. He encouraged me to pursue what was offered.

But to get an offer to run a department, even a small one at another big Wall Street firm, shocked me. Neil was several years my senior and had a corresponding amount of experience on the Street. I wasn't getting his job at Lehman anytime soon. Neil wasn't going anywhere that I could tell, and I was making big strides quickly. I might be stuck for a while. So I convinced myself that it would make sense to go talk to Credit Suisse. That's what everyone always says, "What's the harm in meeting with them and seeing what they have to say?" That line of thinking is so far from the truth, a lie we tell ourselves so we can downplay our actions. No big deal, I'm not about to betray my boss and firm by leaving for a competitor. Just a cup of coffee and a quick conversation. So what?

I went for coffee. And I was seduced. They offered a promotion, making me head of the preferred securities group and doubling my compensation. In my mind, I rationalized that I couldn't say no. What a chance. And so quickly. Carpe diem! Peter was 100 percent on board, which certainty bolstered my confidence. All that stood between me and this great new job was resigning from Lehman Brothers. Now it seems strange that the person who went to Lehman to begin with had disappeared so quickly. Was I still the person who went there because of the people, since I liked them so much? The person who never even considered working anywhere else? Who didn't even want to interview at another Wall Street firm because I didn't have the personal connections I did at Lehman? The person to whom money and title had not been relevant, as long as I had a shot at a new career path in a place I felt I belonged? Was I so easily swayed from my values? I am sorry to say it seemed that way. But I still had a big task ahead. I had to resign first.

Once everything was finalized with Credit Suisse and I had a contract in hand, I picked the following day to go in and resign at Lehman. I gathered my courage after some coaching from my soon-to-be new colleagues, went into Lehman's offices at 3 World Trade Center, and asked Bart McDade, Neil's boss and head of high-grade fixed income, if I could speak with him. I should have resigned to Neil, since he was my direct boss, but he was in Asia that week for business. It was convenient timing for me because I convinced myself that resigning to Bart made more sense anyway because part of why I was leaving was that Neil would be getting in my way over time. How could I tell Neil that? Now I see that I should have waited for Neil to get back. Resigning to Bart would make Neil look bad. I never even considered that at the time.

I stepped into Bart's office and pushed my Lehman identification card slowly across his desk toward him and told him I was resigning. I'd been advised ahead of time to say nothing more. I'd been universally coached not to say where I was going so that they couldn't talk me out of it. I couldn't fight the feeling that I owed Lehman an explanation. Not providing some answers is really reprehensible. He asked why and I started to tear up, water welling immediately to the corners of my eyes. I felt lame, but I shouldn't have, because deep down I was still the person who loved it there. I was filling my life with work as others did with love and family, and Lehman was becoming my family. Walking away was a bigger trauma than I had considered or allowed for. The emotion kicked in. And thank goodness. It should have.

To make a long story short, within several hours, I had a new job at Lehman heading the financial institutions team in debt capital markets, a promotion to run a small team. It wasn't Neil's job, but one with a lot of skill and content overlap to what I'd been doing, so it was a good fit. They also agreed to increase my compensation to what Credit Suisse had promised.

Other than some mistakes in the execution, this may look like a good story for me. A woman stepping up and taking control of her career to get what she deserved, or at least, what she wanted. It seems like it all worked out in the end, but it really didn't. First of all, all my close colleagues knew I had tried to resign and got offered a very good deal to stay. That kind of news never stays quiet. There was definitely resentment. Also, my colleagues who now reported to me in debt capital markets were doubly resentful, since I was their new boss and they didn't appreciate the way that had come about, which was perfectly fair. To take it even further, some people assumed my whole plan from the beginning was to "hold Lehman up" for a bigger job and more money, and that I'd never actually intended to leave. Although that was not true, I could see how it might have looked like that. Finally, the managers senior to me had to question whether I was going to be one of those employees who is always trying to leverage the company into giving up more. There were those employees who deliberately cultivated a periodic "bid away" to get paid or promoted or both. From the outside looking in, the waters were murky at this point. It was hard to argue plausible deniability. I'd only been there two years, after all.

I am not proud of this whole episode. I hope that is clear. I am not suggesting there can't be good reason to leave your current job for another one. I just didn't have one. More importantly, I had been embraced at Lehman, but I was fully prepared to walk away as if it didn't matter. As if all the success that had happened so quickly belonged to me alone. It didn't. There were many cooks in that kitchen. For the rest of my career up to the end of my CFO tenure in 2008, I never again seriously considered resigning from Lehman Brothers to work somewhere else. I never accepted another offer, or had any meaningful conversations with another firm, because I fully recognized that I was happy. I had it good at Lehman Brothers. Not perfect. It didn't always *feel* perfect. There is always something to complain about. We're human. It's in our nature. And so when those headhunters call they know exactly how to tap into that dissatisfaction and exploit it, however small it may truly be. They know to boost our egos. Someone wants me! They know how good I really am! One of the hardest things to do is ignore all that. Don't let yourself be seduced. I always thought about it as learning to be happy. I learned, at least at work. I realize now that it is not very different in real life. It is easy to focus on our grievances. Our discontents. We can forget to focus on the good and what we really have. It takes discipline, but happiness is truly a choice.

CHAPTER FIVE

It's All in the Follow-Through

DESPITE MY LOPSIDED APPROACH tilted toward work, there really were so many good things about my career at Lehman Brothers, regardless of how I let my obsession with work spiral out of control over time. I don't want to throw the baby out with the bathwater, if you know what I mean. Not the least of the positives of the job was all the travel I did. I have a long history of desiring to travel. Even when I was a little girl, the whole idea of airports and airplanes was just about the most exciting thing I could imagine. Once in a blue moon, my aunt Mary would take my sisters and I on a short trip to LaGuardia Airport, which wasn't far from our house in Queens, just to watch planes take off and land. I loved that. Even my favorite song as a child was "Leaving on a Jet Plane," recorded by Peter, Paul and Mary. I didn't understand the deeper meaning of the song until later in my life, but it fit. I was always leaving, leaving people and relationships behind, and always looking to the next thing. Anyway, if I'd known as a little girl how much I would end up traveling, I would have been thrilled. I realized recently that on just one of the airlines I used to fly frequently when I was at Lehman, I had accumulated one million frequent flyer miles. And it's not like I flew one airline all the time. So that gives you a sense.

On average, I traveled three days a week, either in the United States or Europe. I didn't spend a lot of time in Asia or the Middle East. There were some longer stints in Europe, at times, the longest of which was six weeks in London in the fall of 1998. If I do some rough math, there were probably at least 125 days a year when I was away from home every year over several years. All of the travel was to see clients. From Akron to Amsterdam, Toronto to Tokyo, and everything in between, I went to glamorous cities and hotels as well as to dives in the middle of nowhere (brings back memories of the Copper King motel in Butte, Montana). I spent so much time trying to get somewhere else. When I think about it now, I realize the effect of all this travel was that I never truly relaxed, never felt peace. It was a state of constant anxiety. Am I in the right place? Where's the taxi line? The baggage claim? Am I going to miss my flight? Does anyone speak English? Is my flight canceled? Can I get a hotel tonight? I need one near the airport because I don't want to go all the way back to town again.

I still feel a bit anxious at airports now, and these days I'm only traveling for pleasure. When you're a real road warrior you've got the drill down pat. You're a perfect packer. You get through security in a heartbeat. You know where the best fast food is at every airport. When the weather is bad in New York, White Plains may be the best bet. Chicago is always bad. Always. If you get out of there on time it's a miracle. You're in a state of perpetual motion, strategizing your next step from when you get on the plane (I like to be almost the last person on), to how you manage your spot for the baggage carousel. With all this effort to create an efficient paradigm on the road, do you think

I really experienced any of these places? Did I ever build in any time to walk around or sightsee? You guessed it: no. Of course I would've been exploring alone, but so what? When am I ever going to have a reason to go to Seoul again, or Stockholm, or Portland, Oregon, or Birmingham? The list could go on and on. Instead of waking up early to exercise before the first meeting, I could've gone for a walk, or skipped the treadmill and just had a run outside.

Now don't get me wrong, I am grateful to have traveled all over the world and I had a lot of fun experiences and met all kinds of interesting people. I just wish I could've been more aware of what I was doing when I was doing it. Was I hyperefficient? Absolutely. Did I need to be like that? Not so much. Could I have created just an hour of downtime each day so that I could have experienced a new place? Yes. Even if it was just people-watching at the airport instead of looking down in my seat focused on marking up a presentation. Even if it was scheduling a conference call for an hour later so I could go for a walk, or having dinner out by myself instead of ordering room service again. Traveling the way I did creates chaos in your life, and I tried to implement as much structure and routine into it as I could. I structured all the good stuff right out of the trip. It could have been so much better. I took a business trip to London in December 2008 after I had left Lehman. For the first time, I brought someone along. Anthony came with me. He kept himself busy sightseeing during the day while I had meetings and we spent the few evenings we had enjoying the city. Wow. It really was possible to have some semblance of personal enjoyment on a work trip. Together we appreciated the sights and sounds of London at Christmastime. Who knew?

Even now, I find that really staying in the moment is one of the hardest things for me to do. I struggle to recognize that what is at hand might be a great moment, but only if I pay attention. You can't think about the return flight when you're just arriving, so to speak. My desire and excitement for airplanes and airports has also faded. Anthony and I love our road trips. We drive everywhere we can. We rarely know ahead of time where we will stop; we figure it out on the fly, which helps me enjoy the journey as much as the destination. Since we have homes in both Florida and New York, we make the most of the eastern seaboard. We can stay in the car for twelve hours without the radio on. Just talking, or experiencing being together quietly. Unexpectedly, it's so much better than flying first class to Paris. No comparison.

Sometimes all that jet-setting is the opposite of glamorous. You just can't always be prepared for what comes up. I'm actually shocked that more things didn't go wrong during my travels, but some stuff did happen now and then. Occasionally, I had to do a one-day trip to Europe. It sounds painful and it could be, but in some ways you never reset your body clock at all, so it wasn't that big a disruption. Granted, that's the only positive I can think of. One of these one-day trips involved a meeting at Allied Irish Bank in Dublin. It was an important meeting because the bank had been clear about their intention to raise capital, and this was Lehman Brothers' opportunity to pitch the business as a firm. Normally it would have been a longer trip, but it came up pretty last minute, and I had to be back in the States for another meeting the next day, so there was no leeway on time. Funny how that always seemed to be the case.

I flew out from New York in the evening on a red-eye flight and landed around 6 a.m. local time in Dublin. The meeting was scheduled for 9:30 a.m. or so, and then I would get back on another plane around 1 p.m., so I could be back in New York that evening. Sleeping would be on the plane, as it always was when I flew to Europe. I remember feeling lucky because I'd landed on time, was through customs and immigration fast, and was at the Shelburne Hotel in Dublin by 7:30. In these scenarios, I would have a hotel room reserved from the night before so that I could at least take a shower. On this trip, I even had enough time to take a quick catnap. I was exhausted when I woke up and I knew something was wrong right away. My left eye was killing me. There must've been some kind of tear in my contact. I desperately tried to take it out as fast as I could. I got it out, but my eyes looked a lot worse for wear. Still, I breathed a huge sigh of relief for a brief moment. But then it dawned on me. I had no extra contact lens with me. No glasses either. I always had both when I went somewhere overnight, but this was like a day trip. There and back in twenty-four hours.

What's important to know for this story is that I have horrific eyesight. Like if you were two feet in front of me, I wouldn't be sure you were there without corrective lenses. I was officially legally blind. But more accurately, I just couldn't function without my contacts. Having one in without the other was no help. It was like looking in the mirror of a funhouse. Maybe I was marginally more functional than without any lenses, but not much. So now I've flown all the way to Ireland to be the point person in a very important meeting, and I can't see. It's hard to talk and have a conversation when you can't see, let alone read a client's attention or body language. I would be totally useless. What was I going to do?

I called down to the front desk of the hotel with a sense of rising panic, "Are there any eye doctors nearby?" They passed me on to the concierge. He had a name for a reference but he reminded me it was only 8 a.m. The doctor was unlikely to be in until nine. How could I go there at nine and make my meeting at nine thirty in time? Who knows if it would be any use anyway? My contact lens prescription was a negative 8. Most doctors probably wouldn't have that on hand. All I could think was I needed to spring into action. I got the address, got dressed, and walked out the front of the hotel. It was only three blocks away, but that was still an adventure because I had to move slowly. I couldn't see a damn thing.

Somehow, miraculously I see a shop window and someone inside. Of course, I could be no further than a few feet away to figure this out. It was the right address. I can see perfectly well up close, so I'm sure I looked like an elderly woman peering at the numbers on the wall. The door was locked so I rang the bell, and what appeared to be the doctor himself let me in. Well, the long and short of it is he quickly checked my eyes, insisted this was very unconventional, and proceeded to give me a contact lens that worked. I made it to the meeting on time and, to top it off, we won the business. Sometimes, when these types of things happen, you have to think that someone's looking out for you. I had no business getting that all worked out. I was extremely lucky to find a kind and helpful man. I never forgot my glasses and backup contacts again on any meaningful trip, even the short ones. Lesson learned the hard way. Or the easy way, really.

Even when things went smoothly, the biggest downside of so much travel was that I missed sleeping at home. Hotels may sound fun and luxurious, but nothing beats your own bed. And not sleeping in your own bed on a regular basis has its disorienting moments. I often woke up during the night, or even in the morning, not knowing where I was or why I was there. In the early 2000s, I was spending a significant amount of my time raising bank capital across the world. I took several trips to Brazil during that period. During one of the trips, I arrived at the hotel about midday to check in after an overnight flight, and the clerk mentioned that they had upgraded me to a penthouse suite. I thanked him, though honestly I would probably only spend a few waking hours there and it really wasn't that important to me to have a big room. But I would take it—they could have said they were out of rooms or I was in the wing under construction or dozens of other unsavory options. When I stepped out of the elevator and I opened the door, the room was insane. It must've been at least three thousand square feet. It would have made a great apartment in New York. It made me wish I had someone with me. I got myself organized and went out to a bunch of meetings, and finally returned back later when it was time to go to bed. I settled into the extra-large king-size bed and fell asleep. When my alarm went off the next morning, I turned my body sideways toward the bedside table the way I would have at home and cracked my head so hard on something that I saw stars. My body fell back to the bed limply and I laid there stunned.

Where am I? I thought. What hit me? I lay still for a few more minutes and looked over. There was a shelf attached to the wall about three feet high, intended as a bedside table. I had whacked my head right into the corner of it. Ugh, I could feel a big lump right away. Luckily it was the part of my skull covered by my hair, because by the time I got into the shower it was a small egg. I felt a little out of it, but I had more meetings to go before I would board a plane later that day. "And miles to go before I sleep," I said to myself. A little Robert Frost mantra. After managing to get myself dressed, I met my colleague Sandy for breakfast in the lobby before we headed out to see clients. I told him my head-banging story; he had a good laugh over it and we left for the day, but I swear I had a mild concussion. After we got home I would joke with Sandy that we never got any business from those client meetings because I was walking around with a concussion all day. I was only kidding, but it's easy to do stuff like that when you are constantly on the road.

I remember banging my head hard another time in Bermuda. Bermuda sounds like an amazing place to go for business meetings, doesn't it? Yes and no. Short flight. Beautiful weather. There you are arriving in the airport with a mariachi-type band playing and everyone around you is dressed for warm weather fun, wearing shorts and flip-flops and you're in the customs line with your business clothes on. I felt totally and completely out of place every time, but there were a number of large insurance company clients in Bermuda, so I was probably there a few times a year. Most times, I would stay at the Hamilton Princess Hotel, which catered to business people. But when that hotel booked up, occasionally we stayed at one of the touristy resorts on the beach as our only option. I felt so silly walking down the hotel front path filled with palm trees and beautiful landscaping at the Elbow Beach Hotel. That's where my parents went on their honeymoon. I wasn't on my honeymoon.

One last-minute trip I took to Bermuda, the only hotel we could book was unusual. Meant to be a true getaway, the room had no televisions, no radios, no phones. Not even a clock, as I remember; I needed my BlackBerry as an alarm clock. This room was set up for going off the grid, which wasn't something I was planning on doing. The room was comfortable but very Old World. At some point during the night, I got up to go to the bathroom. When I stood up from the toilet bowl, I banged my head so hard on something I fell down. Really? Again? It was pitch-black and I crawled toward the door where I could stand up safely. I saw stars this time, too. I swear I'm not usually clumsy. There was a low shelf across from the toilet positioned a little too close. I must've seen it when it was still light out, but not in the dark. Maybe all that head-banging explains some things, or maybe those are just the kinds of funny episodes you have so easily in unfamiliar places. My head and my body couldn't always keep up as I dragged them around the globe in my pursuit of something: excellence, achievement, success.

If relentless and extensive traveling had its pros and cons, one unquestionable consequence was that all the globetrotting left little room for everything else. By 2000, I had been in a serious relationship with Peter for a few years. In that time, we'd bought a weekend house together in Connecticut and an apartment in the city. He wasn't working at the time, having decided to leave Wall Street for a fundamental life change. As you can imagine, he wasn't buying into this "work is the be all end all" attitude I was cultivating. He'd had his epiphany about his career and decided it wasn't a necessary element of his life and happiness. Naturally that year of our relationship was filled with significant challenges.

The more I focused my energy on work, the more he tried to pull me away from it. It was a constant battle for my time and attention. Looking back, I don't think he was wrong for wanting more of me than I was giving. But as far as I was concerned, I was just hitting my professional stride. In May of 2000, I was promoted to managing director, which was a big deal, and I was running a successful business at Lehman Brothers. For the better part of that year, though, Peter tried to talk me into working only four days a week. Or, at a minimum, working at home on Fridays from our house in Connecticut. I was going the other way, slowly converting my Sunday "just making sure I'm organized for Monday" sessions into all-out workdays. The idea of any part-time scenario seemed crazy. I didn't have children. I wasn't missing concerts, school plays, games, or parent-teacher meetings. What was the point?

The point was that our relationship was unraveling, in part from my failure to nurture it. I also failed to recognize the fundamental change that had taken place in him, or at least refused to see it. Even if I had acknowledged that, his new lifestyle was a rejection of the direction I was headed, setting up a conflict that would have no good ending. Peter tried a new tactic. He decided we should move to California. We were both from the New York area, with almost all of our friends and family in New York. Granted California is beautiful, but it didn't make sense to me. Also, very importantly, how could I work on Wall Street from California? He said I could run my business from Lehman's L.A. office. But, of course, all the resources, information, and everyone who's relevant were in New York. Literally putting me on the other side of the country might be effective in his getting more of my attention, but there was no way I was going for it. I never let the idea take up one brain cell's worth of thought.

Peter didn't give up. In early December of 2000 we planned a trip to Santa Barbara over my birthday weekend. We stayed at Bacara, a beautiful resort on the ocean, and settled in for what I hoped would be a peaceful getaway. After we had breakfast on our first morning, Peter let me know he had lined up a full day of activity. The activity was driving around with a broker to see a bunch of houses. Definitely not what I had planned, but we did it anyway. Although I wasn't big on aggressive disputes, I was unmovable if I'd made up my mind. Seeing houses meant nothing to me, but everything to him. Maybe you won't be shocked that we broke up about a week after we got back from California. I couldn't leave New York. I never had any intention of doing so. The battle of wills was not going to end well.

Moving to California—and the more basic idea of de-prioritizing the role of work in my life—was not a change I was ready for. It wasn't my vision or dream. It was Peter's and it fit his idea of what he wanted for us. Relationships require compromise, and I wasn't willing to compromise my vision of work for this relationship. California was just the most extreme version of Peter's wish. If I had been willing to make smaller compromises along the way, maybe he wouldn't have had to hatch that grand scheme. Eventually, I did learn to make adjustments and compromises, but I wasn't willing to do it in 2000. I decided that Peter and I weren't truly right for each other, so the timing was wrong. Now, Anthony and I have found our own version of "California" on Sanibel, a barrier island off the west coast of Florida. We have a modest home, but it is our paradise. But back then it was work, work, work. Everything else was secondary.

Work kept running along smoothly as the bodies piled up on the side of the road. As things with Peter were disintegrating, and I was heading the financials effort in the debt markets, I moved back over to where I started at Lehman to head the US effort for hybrid and preferred securities. The spot freed up because my old boss, Neil, had also grown restless and moved to work in equities. I wasn't the only restless soul on Wall Street. The buildings were full of them. So if I'd been patient back in 1997 and just ignored the Credit Suisse offer, Neil would have moved on anyway. I didn't have that kind of patience. Three years might as well have been thirty years. But restlessness typically pays off if talent and hard work are in the mix. After only a year heading the US effort, I was named global head of the business. Throughout this time I was working on developing new financial products that were beyond the scope of the mandate of my group. I was always pushing the envelope. I never saw boundaries, and at times it ruffled some feathers for sure. I was "invading" other people's territory, but it was hard for higher-ups to argue with, because my team and I were coming up with good ideas. Clients liked us and we were winning business.

After Peter and I broke up in December of 2000, I envisioned myself on my own for a while. It wasn't exactly easy meeting potential boyfriends when I spent almost all my waking hours at work. So, naturally I met someone else at work. As I've said, I've never had trouble meeting people, it was just in the follow-through that I've stumbled.

About three months later in March of 2001, I met Michael. It was probably too quick, but things happen when they do. Michael was relatively new to Lehman. He'd recently moved over from Citigroup with some other financial institutions bankers. He was divorced and my age. We worked together on a few clients and naturally hit it off. It seems so crazy now, but shockingly, we were married by November of that same year. How did the master of the four- to five-year relationship without permanent commitment jump in like that? As much as I've tried to reexamine it, I still can't say I am completely clear on that decision.

Age was a big factor. I was thirty-five years old in 2001 and it certainly seemed about time. Even though the practical reality of it scared me off, I still had taken marriage as a given, as part of my life's story. Michael also appeared to be very normal, and after having been through some drama at the end of my relationship with Peter, I gravitated to normal. No surprises. And that's exactly what I got. Most of all, I think I had a great desire to be settled, to avoid having a lot of open items in my life. Unfortunately, I think the biggest part of the desire to settle down was so I could concentrate fully on work by taking the distracting process of finding a partner off my to-do list.

Michael was hugely supportive of my career. It was ironic that in the end my career would be a significant part of the undoing of our relationship. Just as with everyone else before, my career's significance to me forced him into a minor role in my life, a role that I was willing to eliminate pretty easily when my perspective changed.

Even with all these factors, I still don't think we would have been engaged and married so fast if it weren't for the apartment. Isn't a good piece of real estate at the heart of a lot of the best stories? And this was a really nice apartment.

Peter and I had sold the apartment we owned while we were still together, and we had to sell our weekend house in Connecticut after we broke up. My dad was our lawyer for the apartment sale and reviewed the house sale. My dad is typically old school, and I don't think he really loved the idea of me living with Peter in the first place, let alone the idea of us buying properties together. He never said a word, but that's my guess. I had bought an apartment with Austin, too, but we had gotten engaged around the same time so somehow that seemed better.

It took seven months, until July of 2001, to sell the Connecticut house and unwind the last sets of strings between Peter and me. It must have only been a few weeks later when an apartment in the building where I was renting in Manhattan came on the market. It was beautiful. I'd been renting in a co-op building on Central Park West and loved the location and neighborhood. Michael and I went to look at the apartment on our way back from lunch on a Sunday afternoon. It was completely casual, mere curiosity. We were not in the market to buy an apartment. I'd been renting for less than a year after unloading the "Peter properties," and really wasn't in a buying mindset. But the apartment was great and listed for a good price and Michael and I convinced each other that we had to buy it. Why "we"? I have no idea. It would have been much simpler if I had just opted to buy it myself, but despite some behavior to the contrary, I always had a couple's mentality when I was in a relationship. You did things together. You were partners financially and in every other respect. We would do this together even though we had only been together a few months.

It all seemed to make perfect sense, but there was still a problem. How could I tell my dad I was buying another piece of real estate with a man I was not married to? I had just finished up with Peter and now I was going right back into complicating things with Michael? Our solution was that Michael and I decided to get engaged. We told each other we would have eventually gotten married anyway, so why not just do it now. It was August, maybe five months since our first date. It was time to jump in the deep end of the pool and go for it, I thought, if you could call that thinking. My first instinct was that I didn't want a wedding. I wanted to elope. The whole idea of a wedding didn't appeal to me. Looking back, that really should have been a Code Red. A bride not interested in a wedding? Michael was fine with it. He had already been married once before and divorced. He didn't seem fazed by my lack of interest in a ceremony or public ritual. He should have been.

So I planned to call my dad with two big pieces of news. I was engaged to Michael and we were buying an apartment together. After I dialed my dad at his office and gave him the update, he was quiet for a moment. He had stopped talking when I told him we were eloping. I had glossed right over it like it was no big deal. But it was. "That will kill your mother," he said. I had never thought about that. My parents might want a wedding, even if I didn't. I guess I wasn't used to thinking that way at thirty-five years old. It had been many years since I had become an adult in the world, and I had long since stopped worrying about factoring my parents' opinion into every aspect of my decision-making. I admitted to my dad that I hadn't even considered the significance of a wedding to my family or friends. Maybe it was selfish. After we hung up, I thought more about it and decided it really was selfish. By that time, I had some sense that I was putting my career ahead of many other important priorities, and this scenario confirmed those suspicions. So I would have a wedding. It would be a quick turn of events, but I could manage. I was a master of execution. I certainly wasn't used to giving my loved ones a lot of my time and energy; they should at least get something that was important from me. And this I could do.

Once I conceded that a wedding was happening, I insisted we do it fast. I understood from years of experience with friends that wedding planning could take up as much space as the time allotted. I had too much going on at work to spend time planning a wedding, and to be honest, I disdained the idea of endless hours spent planning my own wedding. It seemed self-indulgent and frivolous, not a serious endeavor like my job. Where I got these notions I can't say, but they had settled into me over time and were hard to fight. The perfect solution presented itself. I quickly let my friends at work know that Michael and I had become engaged. Jeff, my boss at the time, asked if we had a date and location in mind and I admitted we hadn't even started to think it through. "I got it," he said excitedly. "My good friend runs catering at the St. Regis Hotel on Fifth Avenue in the city. He'll do everything. It will be great." And it was. We got married there three months later and I didn't have to do a damn thing.

The wedding was perfect, or at least perfectly expensive and generic. Because I didn't put anything of myself into it, it came out flawless but totally impersonal. From the wine to the band to the ceremony, everything was just a series of small, efficient decisions. Even our honeymoon was planned to make sure I didn't miss anything important at work, because I had a few deals going on as usual. I was married the Saturday before Thanksgiving in 2001, went to Hawaii for one week because the holiday week would be slow anyway, and was back at my desk the following Monday. We did go away for a second week at Christmas and called it the second part of our honeymoon, but that was a stretch, something we told ourselves because a one-week honeymoon was pretty lame. We would have gone away at Christmas anyway. Oh well. I truly believe that you reap what you sow, and I clearly wasn't planting my seeds in my marriage, right from the beginning.

Maybe it fit that our wedding didn't reflect "us." There wasn't much of an "us" at that point anyway. We had no identity as a couple. It was the opposite of when I got married for a second time ten years later in 2011 to Anthony. With Anthony, the wedding was a complete reflection of who we are as a couple. I enjoyed planning all the details. I wanted to put the energy into it so the unique combination of people that we are would shine through. But with Michael, I managed to turn one of the biggest events of my life into another item on my non-work to-do list. Simply and efficiently executed with no drama. My hallmark. No sentiment, no feeling, no distraction from work. Work was busy, exciting, ever-changing, and that was enough.

CHAPTER SIX

Learning from Your Mistakes

IN THE TEN YEARS BETWEEN 1997, when I almost left Lehman for Credit Suisse, and 2007 when I was named chief financial officer, I had five different jobs at Lehman. It wasn't a totally different job at each turn, but each shift in role was a meaningful expansion of responsibilities, primarily driven by me. I was always clear with my various managers what I thought the next opportunity could and should be at any given moment. And eventually, they would enable me to chase those opportunities, even if it was never on as fast a timetable as I wanted. I was leaning in with a vengeance, pushing forward like a Mack truck. It wasn't a time for fundamental change for me, but a time for reinforcing the unwavering commitment to the direction I was going. Though I worked hard, it came easily to me, and it was easy for Lehman to see the results. They worried about the underachievers, not the overachievers, so admiration, not caution, ruled the day and success pushed the equilibrium further and further out of balance.

Even though I spent years convincing myself and the people around me that a work-centric life was all I desired, there were some blatant inconsistencies in my behavior. I remember sitting at lunch with my parents and sisters one late weekend afternoon. My mother casually mentioned having caught up with a friend who had some awareness of my career success. The friend had a daughter who supposedly admired the kind of life I was leading, or something along those lines. I know I was feeling particularly tired and a little overwhelmed by some work stress that day. Maybe as a result, I had a sharp, visceral response. "The life I am living?" I responded edgily, "I wouldn't wish it on anybody." It was a pretty shocking thing for me to say at that point, leading what appeared to be not just a fantastically successful career and happy life, but a glamorous and powerful one. Either no one at the table wanted to take on my comment, or maybe it just wasn't really heard. But I know I said it.

But, where did that sharp reaction come from, really? It strikes me now as unexpectedly angry. It wasn't yet a conscious feeling, but it was already there, that nagging feeling of discontent that would return with a vengeance a few years later.

In 2003, I finally convinced management that we needed a multimarket new product development effort. The group had different names over time but the most appropriate one was Client Solutions. For three years we kept expanding this initiative and mandate and it worked well. This may all sound very logical, but on Wall Street each product tends to be run like its own independent small business with separate profit and loss tracking and accountability. This one was not set up well for crossing those lines. People had to be housed in and paid by a distinct group. If you were housed in the debt business and made money for the equity business it threw everyone into a quandary. Who got the money? Who paid whom? It was always a huge challenge. My own feeling was that these turf battles were shortsighted.

Because every Wall Street firm tended to have this same construct, if you could cross the lines, you could win business more easily. If you're winning, you'll get paid and rewarded somehow because your employer won't want to lose you. And that was pretty much true. The devil was in the details but success would take care of itself.

Early on in the first incarnation of Client Solutions, we ran a weekly meeting called "The Doctor Is In" at which bankers from all over the firm would come to consult with a multidisciplinary team comprised of members from my group and some other colleagues from around Lehman. The bankers would present a tough, specific client problem and we would try to come up with possibilities and solutions. My friend Victor from syndicate used to joke that at each meeting we prepared by putting on our white lab coats. To me, it was fun. That was the true nerd in me. It was different. I felt like I had tremendous freedom to put my stamp on things, to create winning processes with talented people. And if I knew anything, I knew internal marketing was as important as marketing to clients. If we could get our Lehman colleagues to see my team as a creative think tank we would get all the opportunity we could handle.

It may go without saying but I strongly believe that branding yourself with your colleagues matters. They know what you have to offer and you constantly reinforce that message. This came very naturally to me. You hear the lament often that women don't toot their own horns like men do. Women supposedly don't vociferously articulate their accomplishments like their male counterparts. Though that does ring true in most instances, I had no problem creating a brand for myself. Not that I consciously thought about it in those terms, but I knew I needed to present a clear value proposition that was substantive and unique. It seemed obvious to me. I think, though, that all this was driven by a deeper insecurity, a need to validate myself at work in an unambiguous way because I did not understand what my value was outside of work. All my creative thinking went into work. All my imagination. How could I be better? How could we be more unique as a firm? How could we distinguish ourselves with clients? It was constant, obsessive thinking. I would spend all day with these thoughts, and I would come home at night and talk to my husband Michael about the same things. Eventually, work was my only topic of conversation. It wasn't just with Michael. I did the same thing with friends and family, too, as if it was fascinating everyone. How boring! But everyone went along, letting me control the dialogue. It's not even fair to call it a dialogue when the whole conversation relates to yourself.

Even at the time, though, as with all things, my work life was not all wine and roses. Things didn't always work out. There were mistakes. There were always situations or people you mishandled. The challenge was learning to live with them. Even with a steady upward trajectory, there were setbacks. Setbacks are important to humble you, even if only a little bit. They make you wiser about what can go wrong. Learning from the mistakes and bouncing back was key. It's an easy thing to say, but a hard thing to execute.

With the financial market upheaval in the immediate aftermath of September 11, 2001, I was in the middle of a more difficult and real client situation. I wasn't just marketing ideas to clients, but I had completed actual transactions for them. In the few years prior, I had worked on a handful of deals for Zurich, the large Swiss-based insurance company. They were creative deals for the client's unique circumstances that were profitable to Lehman, deals to be proud of. We had gotten to know Zurich well as a firm over the course of these transactions, and Morgan Murphy, the global treasurer, and I came to have a very good relationship. There were months where we would talk every day as we developed and finalized a few different deals. Several of these transactions were executed in a segment of the US securities markets. When these markets struggled immediately after 9/11 with all of the volatility, the deals we had completed for Zurich "failed," meaning that there were more sellers than buyers at auction and would-be sellers were forced to hold on to their securities at a higher yield. That sounds okay, but the sellers wanted out, not a higher return, and Zurich also had to pay higher rates to investors as a result. Everyone was unhappy, and when or how things might improve was unclear.

Zurich had a brand-new chief executive officer, Jim Schiro, who called our CEO, Dick Fuld, to complain that the Lehman team had not fully explained the risk of this type of outcome. I also got my own direct plaintive calls from Morgan Murphy, who was very unsettled. Zurich not only had high-priced capital, but a public relations problem from the group of investors at auction complaining they wanted to sell. Jim asked Dick, "What is Lehman going to do about it?" To state the obvious, this is a lot worse than putting the wrong bank or regulator's name in a presentation, as I'd regretted doing in my first few months at Lehman. A lot worse. So now I get summoned to see Dick Fuld for the first time in my career, and it's not like he had a reputation as a shrinking violet. He was sometimes called the "Gorilla" and it wasn't because of his soft touch. This was really my first introduction to him. Not ideal to say the least.

I don't know why, even as I sit here today, but I really wasn't scared. It was unfortunate how things played out, but I felt comfortable with how we'd initially marketed the deal to Zurich. It was natural to look for a scapegoat and I understood why various people involved felt pressure to point the finger, but the reality was the Zurich problems were minor collateral damage from the horrific events of 9/11. In any event, I think Dick's intimidation strategy really shook out the lightweights. He didn't respect wimps, and if you caved or showed your fear, you were done with him. He'd move on mentally very quickly. You could hold his attention, however, if you stood your ground and had courage in your convictions. And I did.

I know all of this now after the fact. At the time, I knew nothing about him and just relied on my gut instinct and what I believed to be factually true. Also, there were dozens and dozens of deals failing simultaneously in the auction market and there was no way for Lehman to step in and try to manage the situation. In fact, legally, we could not technically "manipulate" that market by supporting auctions with insufficient buyers by buying the securities ourselves. So basically, Lehman was not going to do anything for Zurich, and I'm sure Dick knew this before I ever crossed the threshold of his office. All he wanted were some specific facts from me so he could call back and have an intelligent conversation with Jim Schiro at Zurich.

After I talked Dick through all the details of the situation and walked back to the elevator, I breathed a heavy sigh of relief. It was like surviving your first tour of duty. I made it out alive, even if this was not the first impression I wanted to leave on our CEO. But, all in all, it wasn't so bad. There were a lot bigger things to worry about after 9/11 for Lehman and for everyone else. None of this, though, changed my personal situation with Zurich. They were disappointed in us and it really bothered me. I couldn't fix it. We had failed them in a way. I had failed them. It troubled me for years. I knew Morgan had trusted me and I felt that somehow I'd let him down. His job may have been in jeopardy as a result. I wasn't sure. There were permanent hard feelings, or so I thought.

Fast-forward almost four years later to August of 2005. I was sitting at my desk at Lehman's offices in midtown Manhattan, busy marking up a presentation out on the trading floor in the late afternoon with the phones ringing off the hooks as usual. One of the guys on my team picks up the phone and then leans over to say, "Erin, Morgan Murphy from Zurich on your line." "Yeah right," I said, chuckling. The Zurich story was part of our collective baggage as a team. I waited a moment. "Who is it, really?" He said again, more forcefully, "No, I mean it. It's someone saying he is Morgan Murphy." I take a quick glance at the clock. It's 4 p.m. in New York. It would be 10 p.m. in Switzerland. Why would he be calling me now? Actually, why would he be calling me, period? This couldn't be good. So I picked up the phone carefully. Strange, as if I think he is right there. "Hi, it's Erin," I said softly. "Erin, it's Morgan Murphy." It was definitely his voice. "We saw you did a new structured preferred deal for Lehman and I wanted to talk to you about it."

That year my team and I had been feverishly working on developing a new preferred securities structure that would work efficiently for banks and insurance companies with the approval of financial regulators and rating agencies. After creativity and persistence, we had finally gotten our structure, called ECAPS, blessed by the relevant powers that be in the summer of 2005. At the same time, Lehman itself had been looking at raising this type of capital and agreed to be our first client to issue the new ECAPS deal. When the Lehman deal was completed in August, ECAPS got a lot of press and we won a few financial awards for innovation. Morgan had read about ECAPS in the financial press and was interested in working on a deal with us for Zurich. Well, you could have knocked me over with a feather.

"Morgan, I have to be honest with you," I said, "I never thought you would want to work with us again. With me again." And then I paused. "Well," he said slowly, "that wasn't your fault, Erin. I never thought that was your fault." Wow. Really?

I'd felt bad about the Zurich situation for years. And now it was really okay? There could be redemption. And there was. We went on to work on an ECAPS deal together that we executed successfully in early 2006. I spent a lot of time with the team in Zurich that year, and this time it was a lasting success.

I wish all of my failures had worked out that way, but it didn't happen to me in my personal life. Troubled and damaged relationships didn't miraculously spring back to life. No one you'd had a falling out with typically told you years later, "It wasn't your fault." That explains, at least in some small part, why it was easier to put work first above all else. Even with your failures, I could tough it out and rally back. That was so much more complicated and harder to do in my personal life. And, in fact, in work I could be the wiser for it, taking the wisdom to the next crisis and knowing that "this too shall pass."

I know I felt some of that later in 2008 when I was CFO of Lehman and the markets seemed to be imploding around us. Don't panic, I thought. Others around me with decades more experience weren't panicking. As bad as it seems, stay focused, calm, and live to fight another day. I thought we could survive another Long-Term Capital fiasco (the famous hedge fund meltdown), like we did in 1998. In fact we were stronger for it. But another day didn't come for me, and ultimately, some months later, not for Lehman Brothers, either. It turns out failure could be permanent and devastating in work, too; that theme was not exclusive to your personal life.

But I'm getting too far ahead of myself. Besides the Zurich redemption, 2005 was a notable professional year for other reasons, too. As a result, I think that year was a tipping point, as if so much good stuff happened at work that it made it impossible for any other aspect of my life to compete. That same year, I worked on another transaction that was off-the-run and very high profile and profitable. The genesis of the deal was a year prior when one of my colleagues mentioned that General Mills, the American food company, had posited a challenging fact pattern to several firms on Wall Street and asked for solutions. It's not very important what the exact circumstances were. What was important was that General Mills was a client we had virtually never done business with as a firm and we were looking for a way to break in. Maybe this could be it. The whole situation ended up coming to my attention in a rather back-door fashion through a chance mention by a colleague who'd been asked about it by the relationship team. I quickly realized we might propose a solution that had some similarities in very different settings. It would be complicated, but after some lengthy work and discussions with my team, seemed eminently doable. And, to our advantage, we were pretty sure that our idea was unlikely to be presented by another firm for the same reason the deal had haphazardly found its way to me.

That was the beginning of what became a multiyear process where we competed with a few other Wall Street firms right up until the last minute in the fall of 2005. It seemed that every imaginable obstacle got in the way in the interim, including a preliminary SEC investigation of General Mills that was fortuitously dropped in June of 2005. In the end, despite many moments where it felt like the deal was going off the rails, our solution was chosen by General Mills, the deal was executed, market conditions were strong, and it was a great success all the way around for everyone involved.

The deal ended up being a breakthrough for me professionally on many levels. It was one of the highest-profile deals in all of investment banking that year. Plus, it was for an industrial company. Up until that point, all my high-profile deals were with financial companies. But most importantly, given the size and significance of the deal, the specifics had to be presented to Lehman's Executive Committee, the governing body of Lehman Brothers. It was a very big deal and I had a leadership role in making that presentation. A moment to shine in front of the right people and another boost to my career. The deal was so successful that in Lehman's Annual Report for 2005, there was a full page with a picture of a Wheaties box and our deal team and deal summary prominently placed for Lehman's shareholders to review. It was a career-making deal.

But above and beyond all the great professional accolades, I know the best aspect of the General Mills deal for me were the people who worked at General Mills in Minneapolis. There were funny moments with them along the way, but one really stands out. It was the summer of 2005, and for over a year we'd known we were the front runner to win the deal, but General Mills did not want to officially mandate a Wall Street bank until it was ready to pull the trigger on the entire transaction. Our Lehman team decided that we needed to fly out and have dinner in Minneapolis with the General Mills CFO, Jim Lawrence, and the treasurer, Dave Van Benschoten, to nail down our role. My colleague Peter was the relationship manager, and we were bringing one of my bosses, Larry, the head of Capital Markets at Lehman, and Brad, the chief operating officer of Lehman. The big guns.

Over the prior two years I had spent a tremendous amount of time with Dave, the treasurer of General Mills. He was a good man, a classic old-school Midwesterner who was very active in his church and spent weekends taking his son's Boy Scout troop camping. I really enjoyed working with him. I had not spent as much time with Jim, the CFO, but from what I had seen he was similarly cut from a strong cloth of traditional values. My colleague, Peter, on the other hand had an aggressive East Coast style that he'd honed after many years as a successful investment banker. Between the drastically different types of people, dinner was torturous. It was a constant cat and mouse game about whether Jim and Dave were willing to officially give us the deal. Moreover, it was an absolute culture clash.

Peter's marching orders from command central at Lehman were to come home from the dinner with the deal in hand, and nothing was going to stop him. This had gone on for too long. Jim and Dave had no intention of finalizing things. "Is it our deal or what?" Peter demanded late in the dinner as we were finally finishing up dessert. I swear he was leaning so far across the table in their faces that he was actually going to be in their seats in a moment. I was surprised by his approach, given the client, but that was Peter. Jim paused and then said very simply, "I'm not from New York." My colleague Brad quickly jumped in. "I'm not from New York either." And that said it all. Jim and Dave wanted nothing to do with what they thought was the New York "personality." The aggressive, in-your-face style only alienated them. Brad got it. He was COO of the firm for a reason. I could also see it all through dinner.

That General Mills dinner reinforced something I'd felt for most of my life. I had confidence that my intuition about people was pretty good, and most importantly that I knew whom I could trust. I didn't believe I was ever too cynical, nor too Pollyanna when it came to trusting people, which wasn't necessarily the status quo on Wall Street.

I wound up as the person spending the most day-to-day time with Jim and Dave from General Mills. They both wrote me very nice and supportive notes after I left Lehman in 2008. They were very clear about whom they were willing to work with and weren't compromising their requirements. I always admired their approach, and when I see someone being difficult or overly aggressive I say quietly to myself sometimes, "I'm not from New York," as my own private inside joke.

Even with the mistakes I had made with various clients and people along the way, I felt better for it once I got a little time and distance. And, generally speaking, those difficult, and at times, humiliating experiences reinforced my faith in my fellow man. People were more patient, understanding, and forgiving than you would expect. The clients on the West Coast road trip from my first few months at Lehman--Zurich, Dick, the General Mills folks--were all cases in point. Perhaps, in a strange way, those experiences made me more trusting. You might think that it was naive and unrealistic not to be more guarded. "You were swimming with sharks," my husband, Anthony, always says to me. But I'm not sure I ever believed that; if I had I wouldn't have been working on Wall Street. It is probably one of the reasons why I'm not there now.

CHAPTER SEVEN

Opting In

WHAT I WAS MANAGING TO DO at Lehman as year after year raced by in the late 1990s into the mid-2000s all sounded great on paper. It looked like I was the exception to the rule. I was a woman not only looking to take on a leadership role in a male-dominated business, but doing anything I could to make that happen. The dirty underbelly of career narcissism wasn't apparent. But as natural as it was to ask for more responsibility and bigger mandates, it was equally unnatural to manage other people. I guess my behavior shouldn't make that failure a surprise. If I wasn't good at managing my relationships with people in real life, why should I be good at it in my work life?

Of course, you can't exactly run a business without managing other people. I always felt anxious and out of my depth when it came to management. As brilliant as my business plans, ideas, and client skills could be, I could be as equally poor in handling the careers and compensation of others who were on my watch, especially the demanding and high-maintenance types who worked in finance. What I noticed in my career about gender differences, if anything, was that women didn't so much lack the will to lead as they lacked the will to manage others—who were primarily men. I am sure I was not alone in this. Leadership could take many forms, but managing people meant some simple things: hiring, firing, promoting, and paying them. Doing it properly involved a fair amount of time and a thick skin. Just for starters, no one ever felt they were paid fairly. No one.

Unlike my personal life, where I could avoid things I was uncomfortable with, I forced myself into this zone of anxiety. I deemed it worthy to work on this weakness if it meant moving ahead in my career on the timetable I expected. I wouldn't even have admitted *it* was a weakness in my personal life.

I had always thought that the ability to manage people was innate. You were just one of those people who knew how to do it well, or you weren't. A hardwired talent. As a result, I didn't think I could get better at it. It was a strangely cynical approach for me because I usually assumed I could figure things out and get better. But with management, I let myself suffer through the insecurity for a ten-year period. Finally, I decided that the source of all my anxiety was a lack of experience. And once I decided to work on it and put my energy into improving; it really did get better over time.

My issues with managing others may all hearken back to the fact that I always thrived in individual performance. I was a gymnast from a young age, for God's sake. Given that, why should I naturally know how to handle other individuals and manage them as a team? I'd never really been part of a team. The gender component here was absolutely a factor. It can be a little awkward as a woman to manage a group or team that is almost entirely men. I don't know any women managing an NFL or NBA team, and successful Wall Street types look a lot like professional athletes. Having a female boss is weird for you and for them. It takes time to adjust. I had to keep treading water in the deep end while I learned to swim. Stay afloat and come up with a better way.

Over time I did get better at it. More comfortable, less anxious. I gave a shit. It mattered because it was prerequisite to moving forward at work. I paid more attention to my team and what I thought was good for them. I saw us as a real team that I had a responsibility for, not just for winning business and profit success, but for the people themselves. As human beings I wanted them happy and satisfied, at least in the workplace. I don't want to overstate it; management would never end up being among my top skills. But I got better and I felt good about it. I got excited about what we could do as a group rather than just what I could do by myself. I learned to love creating a vision and getting the team's passion for it to match my own.

It is hard to understand now why I wouldn't have applied that thinking to the rest of my life. But by that point in my career, I had slipped so far out of balance that it never would have occurred to me. I've heard that for certain actors, life only exists when the cameras are on. At that point it was almost like that for me with work. Everything outside of work became truly ancillary. Just makeup, costumes, going over your lines until you stepped back into the white-hot lights and the cameras rolled. That was the real deal. These days, there are no bright lights. No cameras. No constant prepping for the appearance on the big stage. My conversations are about real life. About family. About all the ordinary and extraordinary things that happen in every-day life. Before, I thought I was interesting because of what I did for a living and how well I did it. I found it endlessly intriguing, so why wouldn't everyone else? It was so unusual. Distinctive. And now I im-agine there were plenty of people who probably thought I was a real jackass. I totally get that. It wasn't the entire substance of who I was, though. I just needed to peel back a few of the layers of the onion to get to the better part. And people who have come into my life more recently—who didn't really know the old Erin—like the stripped-down version. The rest is mythology.

Even as I traveled tirelessly through that first decade of my career at Lehman, I was still in the office sometimes. There were always the transactions to be executed and the preparations for the next group of meetings. And, of course, the management responsibilities that were growing. It was an endless cycle and when I was in the office, time felt precious, and the experience was frenetic. Those precious hours to get ready for the next client meeting and the next trip. In the midst of all the client activity that was happening in 2005 including Zurich and General Mills, I received a request to have lunch with Joe Gregory, the president of Lehman at the time. I knew Joe very casually over the years, never having had much meaningful interaction. We certainly didn't have any real relationship at that point. So when the request came to my assistant for lunch, I didn't quite know what to make of it. I knew I'd find out soon enough, though, and was okay with that. The purpose of the lunch was not something I had anticipated. A few years prior, around 2003, Lehman had launched a women's network named WILL, an acronym for Women's Initiatives Leading Lehman. I was aware of the network, but I had not participated in any material way. Honestly, I wasn't even sure what WILL was all about or what it was trying to accomplish, and I hadn't seen it as particularly relevant to my life or career, even as one of the most successful, senior women in the firm. It was every man and woman for himself or herself in my head. I'd never thought about it any other way, and I was navigating the waters just fine.

It turned out that the point of the lunch was to ask me to co-head the WILL network for Lehman Brothers. Joe wanted to cycle in new leadership every two years and he felt it was critical to have someone on the production side of the business in leadership. Someone like me, who was a respected head of a business with a client interface and revenue responsibility. My soon-to-be co-head of WILL, Patricia, was from the administrative side of the firm, so between us, we had the bases covered in terms of representing the female population of employees. I remember being somewhat flattered at the time, but really didn't see the whole thing as a big deal. I had no clue as to what was involved other than some figurehead responsibilities. I definitely didn't expect it to interfere with my day job. I really underestimated expectations.

In the early days, as this new role got off the ground, I mentioned to some colleagues I was going to a WILL meeting. We were starting to transition from the old leadership to Patricia and myself. My colleague Greg, who was a good friend, teased me, "Oh yeah. A WILL meeting. That's where you go to talk about how much you hate men, right?" He laughed somewhat awkwardly and walked away. I knew he was joking. Sort of. Greg was and continued to be a big supporter of mine throughout my career. He was usually on my side, but that comment made me realize what the men I worked with thought a women's network was all about: an organized way for women to get together and bash men. It wasn't everyone, but that feeling was lurking. It was good to know that early on, because I saw that more clearly later, once I was fully engaged in the group's mission. Which was, of course, trying to help women, not hurt men. We wanted to help women take ownership of and have full accountability for the things they wanted, not place blame for the things they didn't have. There was a big perception problem that needed to be fixed. I understood the wariness on some level. If you can't be part of it, maybe it's against you.

In any event, it became painfully clear very quickly that heading WILL would involve a lot of time and energy. My initial approach of an hour or so a week for a catch-up and a planning meeting wasn't going to cut it. Meetings and events were constantly popping onto my calendar like a case of poison ivy. Every time I turned around, it spread somewhere else. The itch that demanded to be scratched. Inevitably, I was telling my assistant to cancel my attendance at a WILL meeting and let the other women know I would be traveling or at a client meeting. In those first few months I probably attended less than half of what I was requested to attend. As far as I was concerned, this was a sideshow to my day job, maybe a second or third order priority. And if I was letting my clients and my workload trump my personal relationships, I was certainly letting those work commitments trump WILL. I didn't see a problem with that. Between my co-head, Patricia, the other women who had divisional responsibilities, and the prior heads, there were plenty of cooks in the kitchen.

Treading water in my leadership of WILL didn't last very long. After a few months of doing as little as possible, I got a call from Anne, the head of diversity at Lehman who was also a prior head of WILL. She asked to get together. When I arrived in her office she got straight to the point. Her basic message was that I wasn't doing my part for WILL, given my leadership role. She made no bones about it. Either step up or step down, to put it simply. And she was 100 percent right. My effort was completely half-assed, the same way I treated life outside of my job.

As I think about this today, I truly respect what Anne said to me. It took nerve. I was no lightweight in the firm at the time, and she gave me pretty pointed criticism. The more I think about it the more I wish there'd been more people around me like that. I didn't need more of them in my work life. I needed them in my personal life. As long as WILL ranked low on the list of my to day-to-day responsibilities, it would always suffer. I heard her and I really wasn't defensive about it because it had been a conscious decision on my part to de-prioritize WILL. But as I listened to her I decided that I didn't want to step down. I thought I could make a difference, and it was wasteful to forgo that chance. I told Anne to count me in. I would make WILL a priority equal to my other work responsibilities. I would treat WILL meetings like client meetings: cancelable only in dire circumstances. I wanted to do it right.

I am happy to say that I really did do it right for the next two years. I gave WILL a tremendous amount of time, thought, and attention. It's strange that a very simple and direct request was all it took, because it truly makes me wonder if that's all I needed in my personal life. A basic offer: Are you in or are you out? Act accordingly. Anthony has put that question to me every day for most of our seven-year relationship. "Are you all in?" he queries consistently. He needs to hear my answer and I need to say it. I am. Maybe my ex-husband Michael never really put that question out there because he was worried about what I would say. I have to believe it occurred to him, and that he didn't want the answer, either consciously or subconsciously. Eventually, he got it anyway. Before that, Peter never put it in such simple terms, but that question was still ever present in our relationship. And I'd opted out.

How I handled WILL also helps answer an important hypothetical question I have had over the years. Could I have been just as successful, a CFO or something comparable, with a less extreme approach? The time and energy I gave to WILL was not insignificant, but my job didn't suffer. I was flourishing in my career. This evidence points to the answer that I feel in my heart of hearts today. If I'd done things a little differently, changed the paradigm between work and home, it could have worked. Maybe it's anecdotal evidence, but it's a reason to hope.

The entirety of my experience with WILL was extremely fulfilling. I learned a tremendous amount about other women, their careers, and their lives. I also made very good friends. On average, WILL probably added an hour to my workday everyday, though some periods of time around big events were much more hectic. Unfortunately, that extra hour ultimately didn't usually come out of the hide of my regular work. It just meant more time at work and less time at home, another element adding to the slow deterioration of the existence of Erin outside of Lehman. It's ironic that my commitment to a women's network, whose goal in part was to help women balance a fulfilling work and personal life, managed to skew the scales for me further.

But the beauty of the mandate of WILL at Lehman was the freedom to really run it as I saw fit. I looked at it the same way I looked at running my business, thinking about how to be creative and thoughtful to make the biggest impact on our constituency. We tried to make it as grassroots as possible, revisiting existing programs and events and considering how to improve them. If WILL didn't really serve the needs of women in the firm, what was the point?

I have a lot of opinions about women's networks from these experiences with WILL. What I feel most strongly about is the need to make them as personal as possible. The people involved, settings, and topics needed to be close to home to be relevant. It was just as critical not to make anything to do with the network a burden or further obligation to a woman's workday. The worst thing was to make women feel like they had to stay at work after they already had a long day, even if that was what I was doing myself. They weren't neglecting their career if they had other priorities. Also, I never loved the idea of the word *network*. It felt like you were standing at a cocktail party making useful acquaintances. The true idea was to learn from each other and help each other. Finally, we had to be inclusive of men. Make them part of it. Not alienated. Not the man-hater's club that Greg joked about. Whether as mentors or speakers, it didn't matter. Give them a vested stake in the success of our effort. My mentors in my career had always been men. Let them help show us the way.

WILL turned into a real passion of mine. It gave me a forum and a means to exercise leadership on topics much bigger than myself, and that was good for me. I also started to see myself as role model for other women, and understand how powerful that could be. Naturally, the younger women would ask about balance and what I did to achieve it. It was the burning question for the ages, and they never guessed the real truth. I looked so normal on the surface, as if I was pulling it off. I wasn't trying to fool anybody; it just seemed that I had it figured out. Even if looks were deceiving, I was clear in my words. If asked, I was always very direct in my response that I hadn't achieved any real balance, and I am sure my not so subtle implication was that I wasn't really trying. Because it was true. I wasn't.

Really, the environment and fundamental messaging of Wall Street were totally incompatible with a notion of balance. This wasn't my unique, made-up way of life. It existed all around me. I just liked that world. Just as working three thousand hours a year at the law firm of Simpson Thacher had made sense to me, so did life at Lehman make sense. I remember right around this time, a colleague of mine who worked in investment banking had a baby. She headed a successful group that really carried a tremendous amount of responsibility. After she gave birth, she took just two weeks of maternity leave and was already back at work. I was told this by a male friend of mine who relayed this news with a sense of admiration. "Wow, only two weeks and she's back. That's amazing," he said. The sad part is at the time I didn't disagree. I was impressed. Now that's the way to have a baby, I thought. It didn't interfere at all. She didn't fall behind with clients. It was like a long vacation.

I know now how screwed up my thinking was, but I wasn't alone. It was a badge of honor. I think many of my colleagues, male and female, saw it this way. And, yeah, it was not a problem to be successful as a woman if you could have kids without missing a beat. This person had already had a few children at that point, and it didn't look as if they'd created any problematic distractions. So when I say work-life balance wasn't really something I was striving for, understand that there was context to that behavior. Support for imbalance. And I only had to worry about my romantic relationships at this point. The whole baby thing is another kettle of fish. There was no single day in my life when I woke up with the conscious decision that I did not want to have a baby, but I recognize that other people around me assumed that's what I had done. In some sense they were giving me too much credit by assuming it was deliberate. If I was thoughtful and intelligent about most things; that must be one of them. It certainly merited my attention and consideration. But that's not what happened in the least. I just didn't think about it at all. And the sad irony is that for the past five years of my life, the desire to have a baby has dominated my thoughts and actions. Anthony and I have put every bit of ourselves into this effort, hoping and praying we still had the opportunity for such a blessing, that the opportunity hadn't passed me by. It hadn't.

I am looking at Maggie, my beautiful baby girl, right now as I write this. In no way am I endorsing my approach. Waiting until you're forty-five years old to start trying to have a baby is not a plan I would ever encourage. But this is how my life worked out. What I believed to be necessary elements to my happiness and fulfillment changed fundamentally in my forties. I wish I'd been more conscious and aware sooner, but there is a bit of better late than never. We have been fortunate. We will never forget that we have been blessed by the miracle of Maggie. Even with all my misguided ambition, God and the universe have allowed me to finally get it worked out. Anthony was right. I guess I was Derek Jeter.

CHAPTER EIGHT

No Interference

BY THE MID-2000s, about ten years into my career at Lehman, work was absolutely at full throttle. Somehow I'd managed to keep turning it up another notch each year. By the decade mark, I was at Level 11 with absolutely no intention of slowing down for anyone or anything. Given the state of my career it still surprises me that around that time was when the idea of having a baby did come to me. The notion isn't surprising in and of itself for a woman closing in on forty years old. Certainly, I was reaching an age beyond which having a child gets considerably more difficult, and might not have been possible with or without the assistance of in vitro fertilization. But it's strange that this idea was developing at a time when my life had become so one-dimensional. Maybe it was a subconscious rebellion against the paradigm I had created. Whatever the reason, having a child was wholly inconsistent with the patterns of my existence.

Once you suspend disbelief and consider there was something about having children that appealed to me, the execution took a different form than I had ever expected. I started to think about adopting a child. I am not completely sure where that idea came from. Michael and I had made no real attempt to have a child naturally. That's more a comment about our sex life than it is about birth control. I was thirty-nine years old so it wasn't out of the question to be able to have a child naturally, or at least through IVF. Still, we wound up going way down the road toward adoption, a distinct, separate path from where my career was headed. I had a good friend at work who had adopted her son through an open adoption where a pregnant mother chose my friend and her husband as a couple to be the parents to the child she couldn't keep. My friend talked Michael and I through the whole process, names, references and the lawyer in Florida to contact. She gave us a heartfelt description of what it meant to have her son, and it was clear that her love was no less than it would be with a genetic child. We knew exactly what we had to do and what to expect. It's funny, though. She never asked me if we couldn't have kids of our own. I am sure she just assumed that we couldn't. Who wouldn't?

The wheels were in motion. As was our usual modus operandi as a couple, Michael and I started to execute immediately and took a number of steps down the path to open adoption. In fact, in many respects, we tended to follow through with ideas too quickly. Getting married as quickly as we did is the perfect case in point. We made several mistakes with our trigger-happy style, and this was one of them. We hired the recommended lawyer. We signed all the paperwork. We worked on our "presentation book," full of pictures of Michael and I and the story of us as a couple. Basically, it was a marketing book. "Please pick us!" was the idea. Michael really ran with all these efforts, because, as usual, I was busy working, especially at that time. He wasn't working. Divide and conquer is how I liked to think about it, although that's definitely a flattering way to say it with respect to me.

It was more like Michael took care of those things I considered less important than my job, which meant just about everything else.

There was one point in the process where my actual live participation could not be avoided. I had agreed to a late-afternoon conference call with Michael and the adoption lawyer to go over next steps in the process and some other key issues. And as I sat on the call listening in my office on the far end of the trading floor for some privacy, I started to panic. I had a pit in my stomach. All the considerations created a rising volume of noise in my head: drug testing of the mother, whether you fly down to be at the hospital for the birth, what ongoing communication was decided, if any, between the birth mother and child. Was I really doing this? Agreeing to raise someone else's child as my own when I hadn't even tried to get pregnant? We hung up after an hour or so and I went home that night and told Michael I couldn't do it. I wasn't ready for it, nor did I think I ever would be. It felt wrong. A complete miscalculation. He said okay and that was that.

We never revisited the topic of having a child during our marriage. As was typical in my relationship with Michael, he went along with my decision and was amenable. But, looking back, I think it was too big a topic for him to just go along. He really seemed content with either outcome, and I didn't understand that. For me, the more I reflect on it now, the more I'm convinced that pulling the plug on the adoption idea was necessary because I didn't want anything to interfere with my top priority: my job. As I look at it, it's as if I was truly trying to be like a man. I could have a child through adoption without any interruption at work. Maybe I would take a few days off at the actual handoff, but otherwise, business as usual. It's probably unfair to men to say it that way, because certainly most men would never think of having child like that. But at the time, all I could see was how having children didn't appear to slow down my male colleagues in their careers or make them lose focus.

You can heap all sorts of criticism on me at this point, and I would deserve it. How could I have looked at having a child as an efficiency challenge? As something that could work for me if I could find a streamlined method to achieve it? Thank goodness I bailed. Not because having a child wasn't what I came to decide later would truly complete my vision of a happy life. But, rather, because given the priorities I had at the time, I would have made for a terrible parent. I might have been a real failure, and someone whom I should have loved dearly, nurtured, and prioritized would have paid a high price. To give me the benefit of the doubt, I guess it's possible I would have experienced some type of enlightenment. Having a child would have made me realize I needed to change my priorities. It would be important not to screw up. I would want to do my best. The new life would change what I thought mattered. A motherly imperative. But I have seen too many others not achieve that enlightenment to assume I would have been the exception. I may have been an exceptional student. An exceptional athlete. An exceptional employee. But at that point, I don't think I was an exceptional person in some fundamental ways.

The whole notion of work-life balance and how I could manage raising a child with the backdrop of my career was not part of my consciousness. I have come to appreciate this challenge more fully only now. I look at my older sister Cheryl, an extremely successful marketing executive, who is also a mother to my wonderful ten-year-old niece Gabriela, and I marvel at how she holds it together. Between the day-to-day demands of her job and all the travel involved, it amazes me how Cheryl keeps all the balls in the air without letting them drop. She has to figure it out every day. There are no manuals, no guideposts. She just makes it work, and I admire the quiet way she goes about it. No complaints.

I would return to a desire for children five years later in 2010, when my priorities were very different. The time was right. I'd come to realize that no matter how much of myself I poured into my job, it would end with disappointment, since I'd made it the most important thing in my life. It was inevitable. Real life is a struggle, but you rarely regret pouring your whole self into the people you love. And for most people, part of the age-old formula for happiness includes having children, making your own family. That doesn't mean it's necessary for everyone, and I know Anthony and I could have a wonderful life and love without children, but as I look at my sleeping baby girl and the angel from heaven I know her to be, I know she has enhanced my life. A game changer.

But I didn't realize any of that at the time. The baby idea came and went. My relationship with Michael was puttering along, functioning well for all practical purposes, but with no romance. It is hard to complain because Michael did everything I asked. He continued to take care of all the other aspects of our life outside of my job. He was the perfect corporate husband. This is exactly what I'd wanted. I think many highly successful career women have husbands like these, who make all the accommodations. It may be the only way it can all hang together. At that point, a few years into our marriage, I was okay with it. And he was 100 percent on board the bandwagon of Erin the superstar banker.

New factors came into play at work as I coasted into 2006, all of which helped lull me further into my work-induced coma. In April, I found out I was receiving an award from the Women's Bond Club of New York. It was sort of a woman of the year award for women who worked in finance, particularly in fixed income. It was definitely an honor and I would receive it at a pretty big ceremony with a few thousand people at Chelsea Piers on the west side of Manhattan. To accept the award, I needed to write a speech, which I'd reviewed thematically in my head, but didn't actually write until the day before, and even then I only made an outline. It wasn't hard for me to come up with the speech because I'd decided to give an honest and emotional description of my career to that point. But because it was only a one-page outline, I really spoke extemporaneously. It was genuine. I saw the video a few years ago and I am still proud of the content and how I delivered it. The real "me" shines through, at least the "me" at that time. Of course, we are talking about the "work me." Like Malibu Barbie, I had more than one version. This one went over well. I think that because it was obvious that I was sharing a real version of me, the speech was a success. I had so many young women come to me after for help and advice. My message had resonated with them. I felt really good about it and I started to sense how powerful an influence we could have on each other just by being honest.

The next morning, I was walking through the lobby at our Lehman offices at 745 Seventh Avenue in Manhattan and I ran into a few members of the Executive Committee, the small group of men responsible for running the firm. A meeting must have just ended and a handful of committee members were returning from the executive floor. Ted Janulis, who ran the mortgage business, called out to me. "Hey, Erin, we heard you gave an amazing speech last night. Congratulations!" "Yes, yes," the others piped in. I realized that they must have talked about the dinner and speech in their morning Executive

Committee meeting because Joe Gregory, Lehman's president, and Tom Russo, our chief legal counsel, had been at the awards ceremony. I think that was an unexpectedly defining moment in my career. In their eyes, I went from being just a top producer in investment banking, to someone with charisma and public-speaking skills. A motivator. A leader perhaps. Ken Lewis, who was the CEO of Bank of America at the time, also gave a speech that night. I was in impressive company. Given that, I really believe my speech and the audience's strong response painted me in a new light for my colleagues. I entered a realm of contenders to be considered for bigger things.

As good as the whole experience and response to the Women's Bond Club event was, it was also dangerous. The feeling of exhilaration I had from making an impact with seemingly so little effort was powerful. Maybe that's part of what drives politicians? I'm not sure, but for me it added a new, not so subtle element to the equation. This whole career thing could go beyond mere individual success. It could be a platform for something bigger. I don't think the higher purpose was particularly clear—it was amorphous, undefined, narcissistic—but no less thrilling for the lack of definition. It was a new type of high I hadn't even considered, making me desire a bigger role, a bigger stage. Another brick in the wall, taken out of the foundation of my real life. I started to think about the evolution of "Erin the Role Model." A new concept. She only existed at work, of course, but since I was in work mode 24-7, it seemed like the only Erin that mattered. There was less and less of a reason to look beyond my computer, my Black-Berry, my colleagues, my clients, for satisfaction and fulfillment. Why did I need anything else? I was creating a world for myself where this was all that mattered.

I'm pretty sure I was right that the Women's Bond Club speech was a milestone in my career because it was only a month later that I was asked to run a new business effort that would involve advising hedge fund clients strategically, developing strong relationships with hedge fund founders while helping guide them through questions related to institutionalizing their fledgling businesses. As far as I was concerned, there was no more exciting mandate. It was a blank slate. I could shape the agenda and pick a team. I was thrilled, and for the first time, I didn't have to ask for it. They asked me. And I jumped in with both feet, without pause. What I didn't know at the time, however, was that there was someone else who really wanted that job. It was Neil, my old boss from when I'd started at Lehman. Everything comes full circle I guess. Unfortunately, when they gave the job to me, he ended up leaving Lehman to play a similar role at another firm. Of course, later the move would look fortunate for him when you think about everything that would happen at Lehman in the next few years. Either way, it's strange how our careers intersected again that time. I mean there were 30,000 people who worked at Lehman. But that's the way it goes sometimes.

If I had stopped and thought about it, I could have been intimidated by the job. Trying to give advice to some of the world's richest and most successful businessmen. Our targeted clients were the founders of the top twenty-five hedge funds in the world. Many of them were high on the Forbes 500 list of the wealthiest individuals on the planet. Every single client was a man. Why would they listen to me? How could I really tell them something of value? I was new to this world of hedge funds, having spent most of my career with well-established financial institutions and big companies. So how could I make an impact? Good thing I didn't spend a lot of time pondering those uncertainties. Sometimes it's just best to forge ahead, to develop a plan of attack and execute it without giving yourself too much time to contemplate the drawbacks. That's what I did.

I had to report back to the Executive Committee of the firm in June, only a few months later, on our progress with the new hedge fund initiative. By then, I had put a team together, a combination of some of the guys who had previously worked for me and some new people from inside Lehman who had approached me with interest when they heard about the new business opportunity. We had worked with all the divisions of Lehman and senior client relationship managers to create a client target list and tiering of priorities. And, most importantly, we had developed the content of our initial meetings with these clients, which covered hot topics in the hedge fund space. It had been a whirlwind effort in a short few months. We started having introductory meetings with our target client list and it really was an unmitigated success. Almost immediately we started winning business from these hedge fund clients. It was a new kind of very high-profile business. It also improved our relationships with these hedge funds across the board including trading revenues and profitability from some of the most important clients we had. Our rising tide raised all our ships.

In addition to profitability, there were a number of things that were important about taking the hedge fund job and how well it worked out professionally. I was no longer toiling a bit obscurely as the mad scientist on unusual client situations. That's probably not totally fair. At that point, for a few years, I had been working front and center with key clients who mattered to a lot of people at Lehman. But now the top dogs were paying attention. Dick Fuld, our CEO, knew these hedge fund founders well. In fact, he did very well with them. They respected him and his style and perhaps related to it. He felt at ease and was confident with them. Now Dick was getting a chance to see up close the effect the new program was making, and getting to know me in a new light. I was on his radar screen. I'd been on Joe Gregory's for a while now for other reasons including my WILL role, but Dick's attention was a different matter altogether. This intersection was unusual.

On a personal level, the job was important in good and bad ways. On the positive side, I learned to work with people and groups across all divisions of Lehman for a common goal. I never saw hard lines and boundaries in any role I ever had at Lehman, but this was the ultimate version of blurred lines. Although I was technically housed in the investment banking division— since fundamentally my role was an advisory one—it really was a pan-divisional job. The most cross-firm role I could imagine. I really thought in that way, indifferent to where the profits went from good work rewarded. As long as we were getting it right with the client, we were getting it right. Period. I gained confidence from my quick success, but now I see it was too much confidence. If within six months of this brand-new effort I had the ear of some of the most successful men on the planet, what couldn't I accomplish? I remember about this time in late 2006, one of the popular investment magazines published a story about me and what our group was doing. There was a full-page head shot with the caption "Alpha Female." That was me. I started to feel a bit invincible.

That's not to say that I approached my new hedge fund clients without some trepidation, in every case. I had some insecurities, which was natural since I wasn't crazy, or completely delusional. In particular, I remember my first trip to visit Ken Griffin, who'd founded the hedge fund Citadel. This was in the summer of 2006. I already had met with several founders of large hedge funds in New York and Greenwich, but Citadel was based in Chicago. So I headed out with my colleague Rob Shafir, who managed the relationship. Because we were flying there, not taking a taxi across town, I had all that flight time in the air to read more on background about Ken himself than I usually did with a client. By the time I landed, I was panicked. Everything I had read suggested Ken was crazy smart, tough, demanding, and didn't suffer fools lightly. It's not like I didn't know other people like this, but I worried that this was perhaps unfamiliar territory for me. Why would he care about what I had to say about anything? What was my value proposition for him? He knew a hundred times more than me about the inner workings of hedge funds. This was new for me—in my career up to that point, I had always known a tremendously greater amount about my area of expertise than my clients did. They were looking for my advice and insight. But I was still new enough to the hedge fund space to recognize I wasn't yet a total guru.

For this meeting, Rob had told me Ken was interested in permanent forms of capital for Citadel, but based on what I knew, he was likely more knowledgeable than I was on the topic. Ugh. I vowed to make the best of it. I certainly knew not every meeting could be a good meeting. No one bats a thousand.

I was way off on this one, though. I was introduced to Ken and Gerald Beeson, the chief operating officer of Citadel. We had a great meeting, but I suspect Ken had decided ahead of time what he wanted to accomplish. He must have felt that this meeting could be productive and I was more than willing to go along with that. As a result of that meeting, Lehman wound up raising debt in the public capital markets for a hedge fund for the first time. It was a real breakthrough transaction for Citadel and for Lehman and certainly a big step forward in the hedge fund world. The deal wasn't without its bumps from the start through the finish, but it was a great way to get to know Ken, Citadel, and its players. Mind you, Ken was intimidating. He emits a strength of intellect and personality that's hard to describe. His trademark intensity could be delivered with a certain degree of charm if he chose. In his presence, you felt like you were in his world. He was in charge. It was lucky for me that Ken had a deal in mind and was ready to do it when Rob and I came to visit that day. Otherwise my guess is we would have had a very different meeting. Keeping his attention would have been a challenge. Content always matters, but timing is more important than anything.

Timing worked in my favor so many times. In the spring of 2007, I remember getting a call from my colleague Steve Lessing while I was sitting in O'Hare airport in Chicago waiting to catch a flight. I had been at a meeting at Citadel and was stuck, trying to get home in the volatile weather vortex that always seemed to control the Midwest. Steve called to let me know that Dan Och and Dave Windreich had invited Steve and I to play golf on Tuesday of the next week. Dan and Dave were the founders of Och Ziff, one of the largest hedge funds in the world, and we had been working with them on a possible initial public offering of the company that could take place later that year. As a result, I knew them pretty well. Steve asked if I could make it. I had a pretty basic problem. I didn't play golf. I had been to a golf course a few times, but even those outings were years before. Honestly, I really had deliberately avoided the sport because golf seemed to turn normal people into fully consumed maniacs about the game. Factor in my competitive drive and obsessive-compulsive tendencies and it wouldn't be pretty. When I even *got* a day off, would I want those days taken up

fully by golf? I could see myself becoming one-and-a-half dimension-
al. Work plus a serving of golf.

It's not like I did anything with my few Saturdays off anyway, so I
don't know why I was so reluctant. I basically worked out, had a nice
lunch, and took a nap. But still. I had actively and successfully resisted
golf for so long, it was a matter of principle. I am not a golfer! Ironically, I did start playing with Anthony's encouragement a few years
ago, and I love it (seems like a recurring pattern). But back then, I
refused to play golf! No Monday mornings for me endlessly citing the
details of the eighth hole par three at some great golf course, or talking about the latest, greatest driver you had to buy.

I paused on the phone line. Steve was still waiting for an answer to
his question before I went on this little golf rant. And then I realized
it was only March in New York. Too cold! "How are we really going
to play golf in this weather?" I asked hopefully. Aha. A fatal flaw.
Maybe I could get out of it. "We're flying on Danny's plane down to
Pinehurst. The weather will be great this time of year," he responded
enthusiastically. Pinehurst is a famous golf club in North Carolina. It
was the site of the US Open in 2014.

My heart sank. It would be bad enough if we were just taking a car
to some local golf course where I could showcase my lack of golf skill.
It is a whole other ball of wax to get on someone's private jet to fly
several states away to one of the nicest golf courses in the United
States to showcase your lack of skill. "They know I don't play golf,
right, Steve?" I said tentatively. "Oh, don't worry about that," he said.
"They know. And, by the way, you're a great athlete, you'll be fine."
Now a side note. When is the last time you heard that being a really
good athlete would make you good at golf right from the start? Never.
That's how many times, because it is completely untrue. You will stink

like everyone else. Once I really started playing golf a few years ago, Anthony would always say, "Everybody sucks at golf." It was his way of getting me to enjoy it and keep playing. I did. But I had no such hard evidence at the time. So what was I supposed to say to Steve? I pictured the scenario in my head—a few hours on a plane to get there, full of anxiety and trying to act normal. At least four hours on an incredible golf course where I can't appreciate the beauty of my environment because I am dying of embarrassment. And, finally, maybe an awkward dinner and a few hours back on the plane.

Easy for them to say no big deal that I didn't play golf. Ugh. Ugh. Ugh. But on what basis could I say no without being incredibly lame? I prided myself on not being lame, at least when it came to work activities. I absolutely, positively wanted to say no, but I couldn't. The "work is all that matters" disease that was spreading throughout my body couldn't tolerate a no. "Okay, I guess," I said reluctantly. "As long as they know I *really* don't play." "They do," he assured me. "It will be great. I'll let them know."

I had a nice couple-hour flight back to New York to think about this mess and wish this idea had never come up. Now, all of you golfers out there are probably thinking I'm a real jackass. Private jet to play Pinehurst on a beautiful spring day? And it counts as work? Are you kidding? You're definitely not feeling sorry for me, but I really was bummed out about it. I was convinced Dan and Dave would lose some amount of respect for me, and they were among our most important clients. Crazy? But maybe not so crazy. I was a confident person, but I had my limits. I had reached them. I had a set of golf clubs and shoes I had been talked into buying years earlier. They were in perfect condition, of course, from lack of use. So, over the next several days all I could do was find something to wear and hope that looking the part was half the battle. But I knew better.

The weekend came and went. I got through Monday at work without thinking too much about the looming Tuesday event. When I got home from work Monday night, though, I knew I would have trouble sleeping. I had to be up very early to get to Teterboro Airport in New Jersey with my gear in tow. It was a restless night indeed. Next thing I know, my phone is ringing before my alarm even goes off. It was pitch-black outside and raining torrentially. I picked up my cell phone in a bit of a fog. "Erin, it's Steve. We have to cancel. There's a bad Nor'easter. The winds are too strong to fly the plane in this weather." Ahhhh! What incredible joy. I felt like a band should start up in the background in celebration! It was off! It was off! The gods had smiled upon me. I'd been willing to go to the sacrificial altar, but I had gotten my reprieve. I'm exaggerating a little, but it was a huge relief. Looking back, it was very kind of them to ask me, especially knowing I didn't play golf. They were the good sports. I am sure they never could have guessed how anxious I was about it. Maybe now they'll know and chuckle. It was a small event in the big picture, but one I always remember because it underscores my willingness to put work ahead of everything. Even my own inhibitions and insecurities could not win out. I do believe it is important to get out of your comfort zone and push yourself as a person. I've been doing that for the past six years since I left Wall Street. I was just glad that wasn't the day to do it.

Ken Griffin and golf were not the only challenges to my confidence during the whirlwind of eighteen months in which I had the hedge fund banking job. Early in my tenure in 2006, I had a meeting with Richard Chilton, another founder of a large, successful fund. My colleague Steve Lessing and I went to the meeting together with the simple goal of learning about the philosophy and organization of Richard's firm so we could start to develop an advisory relationship. Richard, rightly, took pride in the organization he had put together and the talented people he had hired. As he was talking, he said, "Erin, the best way to describe the people we hire is that we don't hire tennis players and gymnasts. This business is a team sport." Before he could continue the thought, Steve starts laughing loudly and looks at me. Richard paused, a little confused, and Steve explained, "Erin was a gymnast *and* a tennis player." Poor Richard. He tried to backtrack. "It's not that..." he started to say defensively and I stopped him. "It's okay, Richard. It's funny. What were the chances you'd be talking to a former gymnast and tennis player?" But Richard was spot-on. When I started at Lehman, I was absolutely not a team player. My entire experience up until that point was about getting recognition for individual achievement. Adapting to a system where the team was paramount was a struggle throughout my career, and I still wasn't always good at it.

The most important skill I could have for my clients was the ability to deliver the services and talent of the entire firm. That meant that being good at my job and perhaps meant being a good team player, because I had to be able to work the entire organization around my client's priorities. Or at least you would think so, but I found that wasn't necessarily always true. I knew how to motivate others to see the opportunities that would come from working with my clients and associated success, but that's not the same thing. The incentives were mixed because you got paid at the end of the year fundamentally based on your individual contribution. How important *you* are to the franchise. That pulls you the other way toward individual accomplishment, so the balance was how to be critical to getting business for the firm, while not being bigger than the team.

Now I tend not to break many of my experiences down along gender lines, but when it comes to the ability to work well as part of a team, I think women of my generation and older were at a disadvantage. It may be more common for younger women to have played a team sport today, but as I recall for women of my generation only a few sports fell into that category. My high school was great for athletics, but at that time we didn't have soccer, lacrosse, or field hockey for women. The boys had baseball, football, basketball, and more, a seemingly never-ending array of activities involving lots of bodies. There were so many opportunities for the boys to have participated in one of those sports.

It's a bit chicken and egg. Did I initially choose gymnastics because I was inclined to be an individual performer, or were the choices so limited that it didn't have anything to do with my personality? It's tough to say, since I was so young, but my guess is I was already inclined toward individual performance. The result was that the whole dynamics of winning as a team were foreign to me, and I think that was true for many women I worked with. I am not excluding my male colleagues entirely from this, but on the whole they were better at it than we were. None of us women had a blueprint for how that should work. Sometimes when the "boys' club" is referred to as a barrier for women's success, I think a factor is the sense women get as outsiders in this team sports mentality. We aren't necessarily being kept out deliberately, but we are inexperienced with the familiar and natural way men work together. They are comfortable with competing with each other and rooting for each other at the same time.

Most of my career at Lehman I felt like I was going the right way on the team player front. My journey wasn't without its fits and starts by any means, and there were backward steps at times, but overall the trend line was positively sloped. It really was a lot more fun when the team was winning. You could celebrate the wins together and suffer the losses with mutual sympathy. It was satisfying to walk in the door every day and know I mattered to a group of people and that you could all only be at your best when you were working together. It was a far cry from sitting in my law office years earlier at Simpson Thacher & Bartlett with the door shut researching a tax issue alone. Even though I knew it was a true weakness of mine, I think I craved this team play before I got to Lehman.

I can't say the individual vs. team theme completely dominated the context of my career in the mid 2000s, but it certainly was subtly underpinning my success and the evolution of my career and my self in the workplace. A more pernicious and pervasive feeling, however, was lurking on a bigger scale. Along the lines of an "Is this all there is?" phenomenon as I got closer to the pinnacle. Closer to the theoretical goal of all this obsessively focused effort. And there was plenty to be concerned about on that score.

CHAPTER NINE

The Big Decision

IN THE FIRST DECADE of the twenty-first century, as Wall Street's fortunes went, so did my career. I was like Sisyphus, my boulder growing in size with each passing year. I was seemingly moving up the corporate ladder at breakneck speed, but was I really getting anywhere? Throughout the remainder of 2006 into 2007, I was still heading my fledgling team for the new hedge fund business and the successes seemed to multiply. I really had the sense that my "whatever it takes" approach was paying off. I don't mean "whatever it takes" from an ethical standpoint, but everything else was on the table: whatever amount of effort at work, whatever amount of time for work, whatever amount of missed events in my life. It was worth it, wasn't it? This was the formula for great success. Once in a while, however, I got saved from myself. If I hadn't been, God knows where I would have ended up.

When I think about some of these stories about the lengths I would go to for my job, it gives me pause. A question I have been asked many times and one I certainly ask myself is, if I could go back and do it over again, what would I do differently? What would I change? I have thought about that for a long time. And the answer has changed over time. Inevitably, I know I tend to focus on whether I should have chosen to turn down the role of chief financial officer of Lehman Brothers when it was offered to me in 2007, because in many ways that really was the defining moment in my career. If I hadn't made the decision to accept the job, things would have played out very differently. It is a real possibility I would still be working on Wall Street right now. Struggling mightily, I am sure, with my addiction. My extremism. Most importantly, I know I could not have made a life with Anthony if I had stayed so focused on my career. He would never have tolerated getting so little of me. Nor should he have. So how can I think of taking the CFO job as anything but a good decision? It led me here to this place where I sit today. A place of peace and real personal happiness. A place where who I am is less and less defined by what I did. My old life is a part of the mosaic of myself, but no longer the biggest part.

Of course, when I accepted the job as chief financial officer, it was for entirely different reasons. To understand my mind-set at the time, though, it's worth revisiting the circumstances surrounding the offer and my acceptance of the CFO position in 2007. Even if I didn't care to talk about it, I've been forced to in many sessions mandated by the investigations and litigation related to the Lehman bankruptcy. "Please tell us, Ms. Callan, how the offer was made to you to become chief financial officer of Lehman Brothers." "Please tell us, Ms. Callan, when you were first offered the job of chief financial officer of Lehman Brothers." "Please explain to us, Ms. Callan, why you were chosen to be the chief financial officer of Lehman Brothers." I could answer some of this, but I certainly didn't know what Dick Fuld, the CEO, nor Joe Gregory, the president, were thinking when they offered me the job. In litigation, you learn the discipline to never assume you know someone else's motives or state of mind. Only your own. "All I know is what I was told at the time." "Well, what were you told at the time?"

So here it goes. It was sometime in February of 2007 that my assistant mentioned to me Joe Gregory's office had called to set up a lunch for the following week. She had put it on my calendar. At the time I didn't think there was anything unexpected about this request. Joe had taken a special interest in me over the past few years on the heels of my role with WILL, my strong business performance, and various client successes. After that Women's Bond Club speech the year prior, and the success of the launch of the hedge fund effort, I knew I was on his radar screen. I figured this for a general catch-up to make sure that I was happy with the hedge fund job and how things were progressing.

The appointed day arrived and I headed upstairs to have lunch in a private dining room in our office building. Given how many clients and transactions I was juggling at that point, I didn't give the lunch much forethought. We started with the requisite small talk. How were things going? That sort of stuff. But soon he started to drift and talk about the big picture related to Lehman. And then he laid it out. "We would like you to be the chief financial officer of the firm," he said. I was shocked to say the least, and maybe not for the reasons you think. My initial gut reaction was not that positive. "What about Chris?" I said. Chris O'Meara had been the CFO at Lehman for several years. He seemed to be doing just fine. I had never heard anything to the contrary. "We have a plan for Chris. He is moving into the role of risk management." He continued to say something about the importance of rotating people in their jobs so they don't get stale, the same idea for the change of WILL leadership a few years before. I wasn't paying 100 percent attention at that point. CFO? Me as CFO? That's not what I envisioned as my next job. I pictured a bigger job than I had running a client-facing business, which I thought of as better than being CFO.

Let me explain my reaction because it may not be clear why I wasn't ecstatic about this offer and conversation. At Lehman, in my mind, the CFO job wasn't some big, powerful position. At least it hadn't seemed that way under Chris's tenure. The position of chief financial officer and the nature of the role can vary widely from company to company, from the obvious heir apparent to the CEO to a true operational functionary—a chief accountant so to speak. At Lehman I saw the position on the operational end of the spectrum. That may not have been fair because I didn't work closely with the CFO's office, but as a high-ranking employee I know that my perception of the job was similar to that of my peers. For me, this was not necessarily appealing. I did not want to hide out crunching numbers in the center of the firm. I wanted to advise clients, and improve our franchise and brand through a high-quality delivery of advice and Lehman's services. That's how I saw my future.

"Why me?" I queried as I quickly zeroed back in to the matter at hand. I was definitely taken aback and the idea of the offer was genuinely not clear to me. Joe began a pretty lengthy elaboration of the reasoning. As he went though his argument, I started to find his thinking somewhat persuasive. I had many qualifications for the job as he saw it. I had experience working with financial institution clients like Lehman for many years, balance sheet management skills, capital raising expertise, a proven ability to work across all divisions of the firm, strong communication skills, strong leadership skills, and a firm-wide respect for my intellect and problem-solving skills. Well, when you put it like that. I think it would be hard for anyone to hear this many good things about themselves and not bend. The way he said it, it did seem obvious. I started to let the idea percolate a bit in my brain. Maybe it wasn't so crazy. Maybe I could make the role more meaningful, something closer to the CEO heir-apparent end of the spectrum. Something that would work for me.

I was still troubled, though. The current CFO, Chris, was not a member of the twelve-man Executive Committee that effectively ran the firm and made all the important decisions related to the strategy and direction of Lehman Brothers. After I came to see how things really worked up close, I would say that, in my opinion, Dick and Joe really ran the firm, but the Executive Committee was the perceived governing body and extremely prestigious. It was a collaborative ruling body that included all the heads of the major divisions and geographies, Dick, Joe, and a few others. How could the CFO job be of requisite influence if the role did not have a seat on the Executive Committee? I told Joe whether it turned out to be me or someone else, the next CFO should sit on the Executive Committee. I felt strongly that even if I didn't ultimately choose to take the job, it was critical for any financial institution to have the CFO participate in the strategy and major decisions of the organization. He must have already been thinking about this idea because he indicated preliminarily that the concept could work. Still somewhat surprised by the discussion, I agreed to think it over and get back to him.

Knowing what you know about me at this point, you probably realize that there really was no chance I would decline the offer. First and most importantly, Dick and Joe had picked me as the best candidate—as far as I knew—and believed I'd be good at it. They knew the job a lot better than I did, so that was of no small influence. Second, Joe got back to me quickly that I would definitely be a member of the Executive Committee if I accepted. That was a very big deal that told me they were thinking about the job differently than what it had been for the past few years. It would catapult me to the top-tier decision-making of Lehman. I would be the first woman to be part of the Executive Committee in Lehman's 150-year history. Additionally, if I passed it up, what would be the incentive to offer me another big job in the near term? I knew myself well enough. I was restless. I would want another challenge soon. A bird in the hand, even if it wasn't the exact species I'd imagined.

Now as a week passed and I thought this all through, what did I not consider in this decision? I did not consider that there were any fundamental issues with Lehman's business model or any systemic market concerns. Remember, it was February of 2007 and it was still not apparent to most market participants that the financial markets were on the verge of a crisis. Markets were still strong across virtually all asset classes and Lehman had continued to diversify its business lines and geographical reach while increasing profitability. Things were looking good, at least from the outside looking in. I had no access to non-public information about Lehman at this time, or any time up until almost nine months later after the appointment was officially announced. I never knew what was really going on inside the firm until I officially took the title of CFO in December of 2007. By then, the world was a very different place and the hairline cracks in the markets from the spring of 2007 had started to head toward gaping holes.

I also never, not for one second, considered what impact being the CFO of Lehman Brothers would have on my personal life. Not for one second. By 2007, the erosion of my personal life was almost complete. It never occurred to me to put that consideration into the mix. It was all about whether it was the right next step for me in my career, not whether it was right for me as a person. By then, there was no distinction between the two. There also wasn't really anyone to advise me intelligently about the decision. It's not like I hung out with a bunch of corporate executives in my free time. And if I accepted, I wasn't supposed to tell anyone about it until it was publicly announced—originally planned for May. The full Executive Committee was aware of the offer, I was told, along with the current CFO and a handful of others, but that was about it, and none of those people were likely to have a heart-to-heart with me. Michael thought it was great and encouraged me to take the job, but given we were only a few months short of our separation and divorce, his input didn't carry much weight. So I took my own counsel, accepted, and waited.

Almost as if on cue with the CFO decision, my marriage ended. Between February and July of 2007, Michael and I went from functioning as a married couple to separating with a path toward divorce. Coincidence? It's hard to imagine that this was by chance, but how do you really explain the end of a marriage in a vacuum? Can it be put in simple terms without its own separate story? Ending our relationship wasn't really something I had consciously debated over a long period of time, and it certainly wasn't something I had discussed openly with friends or family. I didn't even really discuss it with Michael in any deliberate or specific way in the months leading up to our separation and divorce in 2007. I told him there were things that needed to change, but hadn't predicted dire consequences if they didn't.

Through 2006 and 2007, as my career sharply sloped to new heights, it occurred to me that my marriage was not in sync. I developed a notion in my head that if I was demanding and achieving greatness in my career, then I should be demanding and achieving greatness in my marriage. Why had I set the bar lower? Why did I accept less? As a logical person, this analysis had great appeal to me, and I allowed it to become the truth in my head.

It doesn't sound like a flawed concept on the surface. But if you think about it, my argument presented career and marriage as two independent experiences, as if marriage and career could be managed with each in its own sphere having no relation to the other. Really nothing was farther from the truth. If my marriage felt somewhat mediocre, I am certain that my own lack of attention to it and the minimal energy I exerted on it was a big reason why. That wasn't the only factor, but it was significant. If I had put into my marriage anything like the time and effort I put into work, it's hard to imagine it wouldn't have been pretty darn good. I didn't see it like that at the time, though. I saw my logical argument that it wasn't great, and that was unacceptable. That idea slowly crept across my brain until in early 2007, I was convinced of the correctness of my view. I think that's common, the tendency to turn flawed opinions into facts over time. And the more I believed it, the closer I got to being able to let go.

Why did I have to get divorced? Why didn't I try to make the marriage great? Why didn't I take on that project, like I would have with anything at work, and make the best of it? I don't have a good answer for that. If I'm really honest with myself I think it was because I didn't think the problems with my marriage were my fault. Who does? When is the last time you talked to someone about their divorce or breakup and they said the responsibility was on them? I don't know if I've ever heard that, and I had slipped right into that common pattern. At any rate, something truly was amiss between Michael and I. A seemingly small event that happened in 2006 never completely left my thoughts. For me it was very telling about how my husband thought about me, or maybe more correctly, how he didn't.

A few years into our marriage, Michael and I had bought a weekend house in East Hampton. We had worked with a local broker who was very friendly, and she stopped by the house in 2006 to see the progress we were making on some renovation work we were doing. Michael and I were out on the East End of Long Island for the weekend with my sister, Beth, who was visiting. I really shouldn't say visiting because Beth and I spent a tremendous amount of time together. We had our whole lives. We grew up sharing a room and ultimately shared friends, apartments and life events. We were always very close so it was typical for Beth to be with Michael and me for a weekend at our house in East Hampton.

The three of us had gone out for lunch on Saturday afternoon and were just returning home in the car when the subject of our friendly broker came up. As a sort of aside, Beth commented that she thought the broker had striking blue eyes. She really did; they were very distinctive. The three of us talked about that for a moment and then Michael said out of left field, "Well, you know everyone loves blue eyes." I don't know why for sure I felt so strongly about this comment in the moment, but it struck me as a bizarre thing to say. Now, you should know that Michael has blue eyes. Of course he does. So did everyone in my family. Except me. I can't tell you what exactly made me ask this, but something about that "blue eyes" comment stirred me and I said, "Well, what color are my eyes?" I looked away so he couldn't see my face. There was a long pause. A very long pause. Then Beth piped into the uncomfortable silence from the backseat, "They're brown, of course!" Michael quickly followed her with some sense of relief, "Yes, they're brown." She was joking. He missed it entirely.

My eyes are green. Not a brownish green. Just green! Not even hazel. Green. So here's my husband of four and a half years who does not know the color of my eyes. What does that tell you? To me, it said nothing good. I wasn't sure how to process what it meant. What did he feel about me? How important was I to him if he didn't know this basic fact? I am willing to take responsibility for not prioritizing my marriage versus my career. But could spending a lot of time at work make your spouse forget the color of your eyes?

There was a deep fundamental problem between us. Maybe we were only just friends. He clearly didn't see the physical me. Now I think maybe I never wanted to marry the "right" person in the first place. It sounds crazy, but it was as if my career took away from my desire to find a true life partner, because there was so little left over of me that I didn't even really have a lot of incentive. And, in fact, there wasn't much of a void to fill. The air from my job filled the balloon completely. I don't think that was true all along. From the beginning, way back when I first fell for Chris freshman year of college, I really did want to find someone that I loved, who was right for me. But along the way, that desire had been eclipsed by the glow of my career.

Maybe I wasn't looking for the "right" person because it would have interfered with the main objective. When you have to work all those hours and travel all the time, why would you want to miss someone, too? Regret working on a Saturday? Not sleeping in your own bed? Keep it simple. I am not suggesting at all that any of this was conscious thought, but when I look back, I have to wonder. Maybe I really married for companionship. Nothing more. I wanted someone to share those precious few hours when I wasn't working or thinking about work, but it had to be someone who wouldn't complicate things. It's a harsh truth that I at least have to consider. Not the best version of me to be sure.

Even though I couldn't piece through all these strands of why Michael and I got together in the first place, I wasn't completely oblivious in this part of my life. The eye color episode is just one story reflecting a bigger theme. We had no romantic chemistry, the kind we should have had, since we'd only been together for five years, not twenty-five years. We never had it. I think this is really why I decided to get divorced, rather than work at the marriage. I didn't think we had the right foundation to begin with. Being extremely happily married to Anthony now and understanding what is necessary for a successful relationship, I believe absolutely in the power of physical chemistry as the anchor and a crucial element of our happiness.

Thinking about the blue eyes, brown eyes fiasco, I realize Anthony is at the opposite end of the spectrum when it comes to his powers of observation about me. After our first date in late 2007, on a Monday night, we agreed to get together that following Saturday. He would be coming off a twenty-four-hour shift at the firehouse and would be free early in the morning. We planned breakfast at a diner near my apartment at around 8 a.m. My sister Beth, chided me about agreeing to have a second date at the "crack of dawn" as she put it. "We don't all look our best that early in the day" was her advice. I didn't care. I was excited to see him again. We arrived simultaneously and sat down at a table close to the door. We bantered a bit ,and at the first pause he sat back and said, "You moved your hair part. It was on the other side on Monday." Okay, so he noticed my hair part. And he was right about it. Eight years later, I know I'm not getting anything by Anthony. He notices everything about me all of the time. I love that. It is so different for me. Unfortunately, there was no brown-eyed girl in my marriage with Michael. She didn't exist and maybe the marriage didn't really, either. That's why it disappeared so easily.

Not only was this a strange period in my personal life, mid-2007 was a very weird period in my career. There were continual two-month delays for when the announcement would be made about my appointment to the role of chief financial officer. Before the announcement, I had to figure out how to handle transitioning out of my current job in the hedge fund business. The team of people I'd just put together less than a year prior was firing on all cylinders. What would happen to them? I had convinced each one of them to join me in this new mission to advise hedge funds and now I was abandoning them. I had to find my successor who could lead the group forward. I also felt guilty about my clients. I had promised them something I was just starting to deliver on and was already stepping away? I know this stuff happens all the time, but it doesn't mean you don't feel bad about it. I felt a lot guiltier about that than I felt about my divorce. Go figure. When the CFO position was finally announced, my clients ended up happy with my move because it could only really help them for me to have a more powerful role at Lehman with a personal connection. My team was a different story. That was a tough one.

I didn't feel right about putting someone else in my hedge fund spot, despite how capable my successor turned out to be. I believe all high achievers think that way. How can I be replaced? I used to joke with friends leaving the firm over the years that the building won't fall down without you in it. But it was funny because somewhere inside of us we believed that it would. But to move forward we have to address what we're leaving behind. So, all in all, the months from February to September of 2007 were a mixed bag. I had to keep my head down and stay the course on my current hedge fund job while planning for my departure and replacement. But I couldn't really do anything or say anything about the new CFO job until it was publicly announced. The original May deadline for the announcement slipped away when the head of the fixed income business at Lehman, Mike Gelband, stepped down unexpectedly—or at least it was surprising from my non-insider vantage point. I never knew the details about what happened with him and whether he was asked to step down or decided to go on his own, but it wasn't a good sign in the scheme of things. I took it as an isolated event at the time. I figured I'd be told what I needed to know. I didn't ask any questions, which was ironic since I was known for my persistent questioning of my colleagues about all things that I felt didn't sound right or needed a fuller explanation. It was very unlike me to be quiet in most circumstances, but I was in new territory. Eventually, Joe did reach out to me to let me know we needed to adjust the timing of the announcement. Changing the personnel in the roles of CFO and the head of risk management at the same time that the fixed income head was leaving might create an unwarranted negative perception. These simultaneous changes could suggest a problem that didn't exist, since the CFO and risk changes had been contemplated for months before. We would wait a few more months until July when things would quiet down and the new head of fixed income was in place for a reasonable period of time.

By July, Michael and I were fully separated, both mentally and physically. Getting divorced should have been a pretty dramatic change in my life, but I didn't allow it to be. Michael had been my constant companion when I wasn't at work. You'd think I'd be down or a little depressed. Instead, I was hopeful during my newly single life, which began in earnest in late June of 2007. I was getting myself focused on moving into the CFO role as the months had passed. From that initial ambivalence I was now officially excited. I had worked with a few colleagues on the game plan of handing off the baton on my hedge fund job and I was getting more comfortable with that notion. I didn't do a lot of socializing that summer. I do remember going to a few dinner parties of friends and colleagues as the odd man out, the only single person in attendance. I was okay with it, though. It felt like a waiting period. Something really good was going to happen, it just wasn't happening quite yet. And I knew it wasn't just the job change. It was a life change. I had separated myself from Michael for a reason. I was hoping for something different in my life. And that something would come by November, in spades, in the form of Anthony.

July came and went. The first cracks in the residential mortgage market were starting to surface. Again, Joe let me know we were in deferral mode for making any announcements, given the market noise. I never had any details about any circumstances specific to Lehman at this time. It didn't seem illogical to me to wait until market conditions improved and it was always the assumption that they would improve. Almost everyone seemed to believe that. The summer dragged on. I made plans to take my parents, my aunt Mary, and my sister Beth on a family trip to Lake Como, Italy, the first week of September as it appeared no changes were imminent. The family trip to Italy was part of the upside of all the hard work that I haven't talked much about. It really was gratifying to be able to indulge my family with a beautiful trip, and we'd done that on several occasions. This was a true silver lining and I knew they were grateful for a chance to stay in a beautiful place, but, most importantly, to spend uninterrupted time together.

By this time, I'd become accustomed to the fact that I would eventually become CFO, but it was not yet a relevant fact for my everyday life.

By the third week of September 2007, I was back in Europe for an investment banking off-site conference. Lehman announced its 2007 third quarter earnings on Tuesday, September 18. My understanding was that the earnings announcement had gone relatively smoothly, and that was why I got a call in London late that evening to let me know I needed to fly back to New York in the morning. Lehman would announce the change in CFO on Thursday, only two days later. After almost six months of waiting, I had about twenty-four hours' notice. I packed up and flew back. There was a press release that Thursday morning, September 20, announcing the change and my promotion to CFO. The broadly disseminated press release said that the new CFO had "distinguished herself by her deep financial acumen and strong client relationships." It didn't say anything about how hard I had worked. It didn't make any reference to the component I had felt was most critical: my unwavering focus and commitment to my job as the top priority in my life. It didn't say, "She has consistently forgone a personal life to achieve excellence in her job." That didn't mean my hard work and personal sacrifices were irrelevant. But would I have been there anyway if I had taken a more rational approach? If I had paid greater attention to the other parts of my life?

It is ultimately an unanswerable question, but I have a strong opinion about it, and I have better information on this topic than anyone else. You don't have to agree, but I know it to be true that I would have been in the same place even if I had modified my approach. I spent so much time at work and thinking about work at home that could have been eliminated. Extra work that probably was not that productive after a certain point in the day, diminishing returns on all of that precious time. Believe me, I am not suggesting any kind of nine-to-five scenario with free weekends for corporate executives. That is not realistic for any of us, nor do I think it is appropriate to expect that lifestyle as part of the job description. Executives sign up for much more than that, and if it doesn't work for you then so be it. Our lives are defined by choices based on our priorities at the time. But there is a big gap between forty hours a week and the sixty-five to seventy hours a week that was the norm for me at that point. Even if I split the difference, I would have picked up three hours each weekday. A lot of quality living can be done in three hours a day.

What happened after September 20, 2007, when it was announced that I was the new chief financial officer of Lehman Brothers, was the ultimate proof in the pudding. Because all the hard work, dedication, "financial acumen" and experience didn't mean a damn thing when the shit hit the fan. And then what was I left with? Who was the person left behind?

CHAPTER TEN

Baptism by Fire

IN THE IMMEDIATE AFTERMATH of the September 20 CFO announcement, it felt like the more things change, the more they stayed the same. I wasn't officially taking the job until December 1. For at least a month, I still carried on running the hedge fund effort and sitting on the trading floor. At least by that point, I could work with my team openly on transitioning responsibilities and clients as we planned my exit. I spent a fair amount of time with Brian, who was taking over the group for me. It wasn't yet clear to me what my new day job as CFO would look like, and it was hard to figure out how to familiarize myself with the new job while I was trying to hand off an early stage productive business that had a lot going on. We were in the home stretch on the Och Ziff initial public offering that would be completed by mid-November. There were a dozen other balls in the air, and of course, to me they were all mission critical.

By the third week of October, Dick and Joe had created a new office for me on the thirty-first floor of our offices at 745 Seventh Avenue. The executive floor. I was right next door to Joe, and down the hall from Dick. They had taken a small conference room and converted it to office space. By the end of the month, I had moved my files and my limited amount of personal effects up there and started to dig in. When I say a limited amount of personal stuff, I really mean it. You could blame it on the fact that I sat on a trading desk for so many years, which limited my space for such things. Still, I'd also had an office in addition to my desk on the trading floor for many years now, even if I didn't spend a lot of time in it. The office was not filled with the photographs and personal life memorabilia other people had. Maybe this is a good litmus test of work-life balance. Do you have enough real life to decorate your office? Or do you have more commemorative deal toys than personal photographs? My office stood in stark contrast to those of my other colleagues. Not that I thought everyone else was actually much more balanced. Most weren't. I just wasn't even trying to fake it. Maybe that's a little harsh. I just didn't even aspire to present my "life." It all took place right there at 745 Seventh Avenue for everyone to see.

The days in the pre-official and post-announcement period of my CFO role in October and November of 2007 were overwhelmed by internal meetings, a relatively new phenomenon for someone like me who had spent so many years outside the office traveling to see clients. Almost every member of the Executive Committee was on my calendar to meet with me, plus all my new direct reports, heads of various businesses, internal legal counsel, our outside lawyers, our accountants, and anyone else you can or can't imagine. The list went on and on. Between those meetings and in my spare time, which came typically after 6 p.m. at night and on weekends, I would spend several hours reading reports on the financial status of the firm. The reporting was daily, but felt endless. Just reading those reports should have taken me months alone. From late October, until I was officially the chief financial officer of Lehman Brothers in December, I spent my days and nights in this fashion. It was the steepest learning curve I'd faced yet, and I'd had a lot of practice at mastering new things in my career. I now had officially reached the most extreme scenario. Trying to be effective in a new job in the context of market conditions that were beginning to falter was less about my approach to things and more about what the situation demanded. There was no apprentice period, no way to get smart and experienced before I was really on the hook and in the spotlight. There almost weren't enough hours in the day to get as educated as I thought necessary. Even the idea of trying to picture going through this baptism by fire process while sustaining a marriage or parenting a child seems laughable. Just having a decent relationship with anyone outside of work would have been a stretch.

Around the same time as my move off the trading floor, I was officially invited to start attending Executive Committee meetings. The first time attending as a member as opposed to a presenter was very cool. I was extremely proud of that. Certainly as a woman, but more importantly, just as a milestone in my career. I was forty-one years old, the second youngest member of the committee, which was a big deal. Monday and Tuesday mornings would always be reserved for those meetings. I clearly remember that first one, though. The conference room that the meeting was held in was right next to my office. At just before 8 a.m. on Monday, the other members started to pass my door and wave hello on their way into the meeting. It was time. I grabbed my notebook and favorite handy dandy Bic 4-color pen that I always used. You know, the one you probably had in elementary school. My organizational skills knew no bounds. Color-coding my notes to represent different topics and agenda items had been part of my system for years. I was feeling good and ready to go. I received a ceremonial welcome from the group prompted by Dick and Joe. Then it was down to business. So here I was, in the inner sanctum. Exactly where I wanted to be. Where I had worked so hard to get. I had my seat at the table literally and figuratively. If I approached this as I had every other opportunity in my career so far, with hard work, dedication, intellect, and people savvy, what could go wrong? I had arrived. It was going to be great.

Almost immediately after my move upstairs to the executive floor and my initial Executive Committee sessions, I had planned to go to London. I had pegged the week of October 29 for meeting with business heads in the UK and Europe with some direct and indirect reports. This was all part of the "get educated fast" campaign I was running in the shockingly short six weeks I had until I was officially on the job as CFO. Only a few days prior to leaving for the trip, however, it became very clear to me that a jaunt to London for several days might be a bit of a luxury I couldn't afford, and I needed to stay focused on learning the ropes in New York. I was familiarizing myself with the key people, and most importantly, continuing to try to get my arms around the reams of financial data that came my way every day. I was swimming in a sea of information and just trying to keep my head above water. I can't say I was overwhelmed in an unmanageable way, but I could see that even though I tended to fire on all cylinders 100 percent of the time when it came to work, that type of effort was the bare minimum required now. The new role upped the ante. It was like training for a marathon, increasing the miles each week as your endurance picked up. So if I had tipped the scales of priorities in my life dramatically toward work slowly but surely over the prior fifteen years, now it was as if I'd dropped a boulder on it and shattered the whole scale. I was sinking to a place that would be hard to recover from.

Why was this okay? Why did I accept all of this? Looking back, it's the obvious question. Well, first of all, there was no question I wasn't going to follow through on the CFO job once I'd accepted it, no matter what it brought. No chance. That it brought a ridiculously steep learning curve in a compressed period of time and corresponding amount of inexhaustible work should be no real surprise. Very little sleep was a given. A permanent sore throat was one of the consequences, a by-product of my of being run down consistently. Even if market conditions had stayed accommodative, those facts would have been the same. The state of the market and Lehman's situation just made it that much harder. The pressure increased, and that is putting it mildly. It was the end of 2007, remember. The cracks in the system were becoming fault lines, deeper and more permanent. Really, I was okay with throwing myself into the job because it was all that mattered to me. You're willing to make big sacrifices for the most important thing in your life. The most important thing to me was being this person I've described. This super achiever. The Wall Street rock star. And, sadly, I didn't know better.

During this period, I learned that only one thing can be the most important thing in your life. I was at church recently where a passage was read from the gospel of Matthew. I knew the verses from my childhood, but I never fully understood its message. In the story, Jesus tells his disciples, "No one can serve two masters." Although the biblical story compares serving God and money, the concept applies to many different situations. As I sat there on an ordinary spring Sunday, this message really struck home. You can only serve one master. It's not new wisdom; it has been a tenet of our existence for over two thousand years, a part of the enduring human condition. That's not to say we can't have multiple priorities or be good at different things, but there can only be one first priority. Isn't this the work-life balance debate, rewound two thousand years?

In the fall of 2007, my master was clear. There was no juggling, no fraying at the edges trying to be the exception to the rule. Now, I still have one master, but it is different one. It is living my life as a good wife, daughter, sister, and friend. And now, most importantly, a good mother. I care about a lot of other things, but motherhood is what dominates. That is merely what I choose for myself, not a prescription for others. It works for me now and that's what matters and fulfills me, what drives me. My complete change of heart surprises even me, but I think I had to rebalance the scales to the complete opposite end of the spectrum because they were so skewed for so long.

But even in the fall of 2007, I was sensing the creeping notion that with Lehman, Wall Street, my work, and my ego serving as my master, things weren't quite as fulfilling as I'd imagined. Is this as good as it gets? I wouldn't let myself consider that the fault lay with this whole life plan that I had allowed to evolve over time. I couldn't admit that it was fundamentally flawed. Even if I'd been inclined to such thoughts, I doubt I would have had time for them; I was willfully distracted as I kept moving up the ladder from job to job, focused on the next rung. I was never forced to evaluate exactly where I was because I didn't pause to catch my breath to even consider it. But now, as the CFO of Lehman, the only place to go would be CEO, which would be several years off. For the first time in more than a dozen years, I would have to stay put for a while. And suddenly, even through my work-induced blinders, neither my present nor my future looked quite as good as I had hoped. It hadn't yet fully formed into conscious thoughts, but in those months after my separation from Michael and the start of the CFO job, I really started to wonder if I wanted all this. I thought I might be locked into a track that would make me CEO when Dick retired, caught in the trap I had laid for myself. I would have to do it, if it came to pass. I would feel compelled to do it out of some bizarre loyalty to Lehman and my own strange sense of duty, but the idea didn't excite me like you might expect it would. The bloom was coming off the rose.

But for now, in late October of 2007, I stayed in the New York office after canceling my London trip and, as a result, my calendar was more open than usual. Since I didn't have meetings set up in New York, it came as a reprieve to catch up. I felt the desperate need to catch up, even just a few weeks into preparing for the job. On Monday of that week Kerry, one of my colleagues in corporate Communications, let me know that Maria Bartiromo from CNBC had requested if I could do an interview Tuesday, October 30, on her show *Closing Bell* to talk about the trends in the private equity and hedge fund worlds. Though I had been focused on the CFO job, that hadn't changed my stature in the community as an expert on certain developing trends in the hedge fund and private equity businesses. After confirming I couldn't discuss any Lehman-specific points, since I was still not officially an executive of the firm for six more weeks, we agreed to the interview. It was way too early and I knew too little to act in any official Lehman executive capacity, but I'd done an interview with Maria in June of that year on similar topics so I felt pretty comfortable with these types of things. I also understood these interviews would be a big part of my future as CFO, so getting more practice when the stakes were lower was a good thing. I definitely didn't see the CNBC appearance as a big deal. Little did I know it would be a life-changing event.

Maria and I had good chemistry from our prior interview so things went smoothly, we stayed on topic, the questions were pretty straight-forward, and I was happy with my performance. Because it was most certainly a performance. That is the nature of these television inter-views. You almost have to go into some high-functioning automatic pilot mode where you field questions and articulate points like a fencer alternately lunging and retreating in an instinctual fashion. It was an-other step in the right direction as I prepared to become, among other things, the principal public spokesperson for Lehman for the next sev-eral years. She conducted her interviews on a balcony overlooking the trading floor at the New York Stock Exchange, and when I was fin-ished, I headed back uptown. I had been back at my desk for a few hours, now well into the evening, and I was wading my way through the myriad e-mails that flooded my in-box every day. But one gave me pause. I didn't recognize the name. We had a pretty good spam filter at Lehman so I didn't expect it to be junk mail. It turned out to be quite the opposite.

It was an incredibly nice note from someone I'd gone to high school with twenty-five years earlier. He had seen my interview on CNBC that afternoon and let me know, in so many words, he thought it was amazing what I'd done with my life. His name was Anthony Montella. I wasn't sure I remembered the name. My memory was fad-ed. He said he was a firefighter in New York City. His current district, in Bayside, Queens, coincidentally had him often driving through my old neighborhood, Douglaston, which was right next door. He mentioned that when he went through Douglaston, he often thought of me and a small group of girls who had grown up there and all attended our high school, St. Francis Prep, together in the early 1980s. It was a very kind and complimentary message and I was happy to get it, a nice change from what was typically sitting in my in-box. I decided to write back immediately. "Thanks so much for your kind note," I typed. I made some other comments and then added, "Which Anthony, by the way?" Anthony and I had attended the largest Catholic school in the country. There were 750 students in our grade alone, most of whom were predominantly Irish and Italian. Surprise, surprise, there was no shortage of Anthonys. Or Michaels, Chrises, Patricks, Johns. I needed some other identifier to clear the fog that had settled in over the years regarding those teenage days. "The Anthony who was in the back of your parents' car after your Sweet Sixteen," he quipped.

Well, that certainly cleared things up. When I turned sixteen my junior year of high school in December of 1981, I had a party with friends and family which included a lot of kids from St. Francis Prep. When the party fully came to a close around midnight, there were two classmates left standing outside: my friend Chris and his best friend, Anthony. Funny that I remember them wearing trench coats, like a couple of FBI agents. My parents asked if they were still waiting to get picked up. No, that was not their intention at all. They planned to walk the mile and a half to the bus stop and then take some combination of buses and subways to make their way back to Chris's house in South Ozone Park at the opposite end of Queens County from my town of Douglaston. That trip would take hours at any time of day, let alone starting at midnight. There was no way my parents were going to let them do that, so Chris and Anthony jumped in the back of the car with me, and my sister Beth got in the front with my parents and we took the long ride to drop them off. If Chris and Anthony had had their way we would have left them on the side of the Belt Parkway at their exit, but my parents insisted on going to Chris's front door. So when he brought up this story, which was part of my family folklore about my sixteenth-birthday party, I knew exactly which Anthony.

Sitting here today, I am shocked I didn't remember Anthony in a heartbeat. He is memorable to anybody who meets him. Really. I don't care how many years go by. You wouldn't forget him. He's one of the most charismatic people I've ever met. Trust me, he can't believe I didn't remember him right off the bat, either. That never happens to him, but that's how it went. A testament, I suspect, to my narrow focus on the here and now. I never tended to be backward-looking. I hadn't cultivated sentimentality in myself. That's pretty obvious I suppose. It made it very easy to keep jettisoning myself forward. I laugh now because when I look in my basement at all our storage bins, of which there are many, and I probably have two filled with all my memorabilia from my life that I saved over twenty plus years. Anthony must have thirty bins. We are certainly different in this regard, although I've started saving more. Maybe someday I'll get to ten bins. Thirty seems like a real long shot.

That's how the man I love with all my heart came into my life. Does it seem like really bad timing? It was only a few weeks before I officially started in the capacity of CFO of Lehman. My work-life balance had almost completely disappeared, flickering totally out in that month of October into November of 2007. I was about to embark on a path that would make a fulfilling relationship a challenge even for someone who had her priorities straight. How could any relationship at that point, especially a relationship of substance, not crash and burn on takeoff? But, on the other hand, maybe it was exactly the right moment. There's always another lens to look through until the picture comes into focus more clearly.

I had just gotten divorced because I'd found my personal life vaguely dissatisfying. I was beginning to openly question myself about whether my lifelong path was the one I wanted to be on. As confident as I had been, I was feeling a bit insecure as I stepped into a new, daunting role at work. Maybe this was the perfect moment. I was uniquely vulnerable. I was ready. And as unlikely a combination as we looked on paper—a firefighter and a high-finance executive—we were perfect for each other. Within a few months, I felt that this was it. I'd finally found the "right" person, even if I hadn't been looking for him. Or maybe I should say he found me. And he wound up saving me from myself at my darkest moments a little over a year later. When I didn't know how to process how everything I had worked for came crashing down around me. When I didn't know what my life was without work and my good reputation. He loved me. For so much more of what I was than I knew existed. Or forgot existed. That's what saved me. He's why I'm still here.

Although Anthony coming into my life was a game changer, there were some other events in late 2007 that were important that didn't seem so relevant then, but are painfully obvious now. A few weeks later, on November 29, a breaking news story came across CNBC. Like my other colleagues, CNBC full-time on a small television in my office. The story was about Morgan Stanley, one of our competitors. A few weeks before, in the wake of a precipitous drop in the prices of certain mortgage securities, Morgan Stanley had taken a $3.7 billion loss on its subprime mortgage portfolio. As a result, Zoe Cruz, a woman who was copresident (and potential future CEO) of Morgan Stanley, was fired because that portfolio of securities was on her watch. In the division of responsibilities, she was responsible for all trading and risk operations, and the mortgage securities division was one of many that ultimately reported to her. In the scheme of Wall Street at the time, Zoe was among the two or three women who had one of the highest-ranking jobs on Wall Street. She'd been portrayed as a protégée of John Mack, the CEO of Morgan Stanley at the time. She had a reputation as no-nonsense, very smart, and she clearly had an exceptional career.

So Zoe got canned, targeted to take the fall for the poor risk decisions of the trading division in fixed income. It was clear that her firing was a shock inside and outside of Morgan Stanley. As I was trying to take in the story's details and process the possibility that maybe Morgan Stanley had more losses and what that might mean for Lehman, Joe Gregory popped into my office. "Did you see the Morgan Stanley news?" he asked with a slight breathlessness. "The news about Zoe?" He was obviously agitated. "Yes," I say. "I just put a call down to the [trading] floor to get their feedback and what they're hearing." The trading floor was always the best source for all breaking news. Information spread like wildfire from desk to desk across Wall Street. Certainly this type of information would be a hot topic, since it involved one of the Street firms itself. If CNBC had the story, the traders had already each had five conversations about it and picked up valuable tidbits. "Okay. Good idea," said Joe. "I'll let you know what I hear," I replied as I started to dig back into one of the daily financial reports and focus again on the mortgage portfolio. Joe stood there for another minute and then he looked at me closely, "Are you okay?" he asked. And without missing a beat I responded, "Yeah, of course. But I need to spend some more time on our exposure and hedges. I'll work with the fixed income guys." "Good," he said. He paused another minute, but said nothing and retreated back to his office.

Now this all seems a bit innocuous, but there was a subtext. Joe had asked me if I was okay with emphasis and sentiment. That went over my head at the time because my synapses were firing on what needed to be done next. I had to understand Lehman's circumstances if Zoe's firing reflected another steep price decline in the mortgage market, and how to mitigate any collateral damage. But I think Joe was talking about something else. Why did he wonder if I was okay? It didn't have anything to do with me. Or did it? Zoe's destiny was my possible destiny. Her story was similar to my story in a big picture way. Did he know it, even then? Did he see a likely outcome? Or just a possible one? It was still barely November of 2007, before I was even officially the CFO of Lehman Brothers, for God's sake. Did Zoe's story foreshadow the story of my career? It never entered my thoughts at the time, but why did a simple "Are you okay?" stay with me all these years when so many other similar conversations have been forgotten? Joe knew something. I was too naive to grasp it, or had instead gone into self-preservation mode to guard against it. It didn't occur to me that things might end badly for me, as they had for Zoe.

So things were not exactly going smoothly around my start date of December 1, 2007. Chaos and randomness seemed to be breaking out all around me. When I think back to the short six months of my life that followed, it's a drastically blurred memory. I can remember specific facts of what happened and who said what to whom; I've had to spend so much time on those details in the past six years of litigation, I could recite them as I sleep. ("Yes, on March17, 2008, I was responsible for announcing the first quarter 2008 results of Lehman Brothers.") But when it comes to remembering what it actually felt like waking up every day during those six months, that's much harder to put my finger on. I know I have a very good memory, so I either subconsciously choose to keep the memory just out of reach or I was operating in such a trancelike state of extreme focus that there's not much "feeling" to remember. I think it's a bit of both.

One thing I do remember is the sense that I had a shocking lack of control over the state of Lehman Brothers and its financial health. Maybe that seems like it would be obvious, but it felt very strange and alarming to me. I was used to running businesses where the decisions I was making every day had real consequences. The market environment itself was always a wild card in terms of how quickly the profitability of those decisions could be realized, but I had the ability to create a respected, highly competent business under any circumstances. I also controlled who was hired and fired and how they represented the business and its philosophy, which was a real luxury, I see in retrospect. But as I stepped into the CFO role in December, the main issue was that all the decisions had been already made by others, and the multitude of five years' worth of decisions had led to all the assets that were sitting on Lehman's balance sheet.

As the market turmoil began to unfold at the outset of my tenure, I spent a fair amount of time in December and January meeting with investors and analysts and taking the temperature of the outside constituency regarding the state of Lehman Brothers. I was actually in an ideal position to get candid feedback, since none of these players associated me with the decisions that had brought Lehman to its current state, leaving me open to field constructive criticism and observations. I came to understand how the mere existence of a concentrated portfolio of mortgage assets on our balance sheet was a big problem, regardless of any quality or hedging arguments that might be made.

By late January of 2008, when I was fully committed to the view that some assets should be sold regardless of our opinion of their future profitability, then my complete lack of control and influence came home to roost. It was one thing to live with legacy decisions that had defined the position of the firm, but it was another to not be able to convince Dick and Joe that we had to move quickly to reduce our positions, even if that meant selling at a loss. Since they had been part of those initial decisions, they were vested, not willing to abandon ship with the same urgency.

It seems to me the reason Dick and Joe were hesitant to sell assets in those first few months of 2008 was that they never imagined the market could continue to spiral down the way it ultimately did, across all categories of assets. My thirteen years in the business did not stack up to the forty years each that Dick and Joe each had. What did I know? I respected their experience, but what I did know is what investors were telling me. They wanted us to get out of a meaningful portion of the mortgage and real estate assets, and get the firm's balance sheet to a more manageable, less concentrated place. And to me, if that's what others saw when they looked at us, then that's what had to happen. Perception is reality as they say. If the perception existed that Lehman's balance sheet was too concentrated in real estate or too leveraged, then we had to change it. We could defend it philosophically until the cows came home, but eventually we had to change it because our business model depended on the willingness of other market participants to lend us money on a consistent basis. If our lenders perceived a problem, whether we had one empirically or not, we had a problem. To me, you didn't need forty years in the business to figure that one out.

I think I wasn't taken seriously in those early months in my discussion about asset sales because I was a novice as CFO. I *was*, and there were no two ways about it. Eventually Dick and Joe would come around to my view, but not until March when the Bear Stearns near collapse frightened the bejeezus out of everyone. Before that, it felt like 1998 when the hedge fund Long-Term Capital nearly collapsed and Lehman was at the center of the storm. That was a storm that Lehman not only had survived, but in whose aftermath the firm had thrived. I'd see. Dick and Joe had been through many storms. This too shall pass. I' d see. And so the Category 5 hurricane was gathering strength offshore, and the thirty-first floor of Lehman Brothers was business as usual. December 2007, January, February, into March of 2008. What was my role? In some ways, I felt like a glorified reporter. Just tell the story. Communicate the message. That's it. Some job, huh? Definitely not what I'd pictured. It was troubling to me, but I had to imagine this was just because these were early days. My role would become more significant, more impactful. I would be a bigger a part of things. And I did turn out to be. At the same time, I was thinking about Anthony. Where was I going with that? How could I sustain our relationship? How could it possibly work out with the demands of the CFO job? Both my work life and personal life were in turmoil in 2008. And neither worked out the way I had imagined.

CHAPTER ELEVEN

Losing My Way

TO THE OUTSIDE WORLD, for the first few months after I started in the CFO job, I was a Cinderella story. A star, young female performer elevated to the upper echelon of a male-dominated world in a dramatic and unexpected fashion. A perfect media story. Even if that wasn't the reality of the circumstances, I allowed that portrait to take shape. As a result, I have a tinge of sympathy when I hear the stories about professional athletes doing something stupid and short-sighted, like spending all of their money in a few years or trusting agents or advisers who end up screwing them. The reactions of the general public are typically less forgiving: Are you kidding me? How could they be so stupid? They've gotten so much so quickly; don't they value it?

In my own way I think I know what happens in the wake of sudden public success. You lose your footing. Without people around you who force you to be grounded, who aren't also swept up in the trappings of your success, it is almost impossible to be your normal, sane self—assuming you were ever sane in the first place. I know it seems so obvious, but until it happens to you, it is hard to imagine how really difficult it is to navigate that kind of good fortune. I certainly didn't handle it the way I wish I had. There was no real permanent damage done, but I've had a significant life lesson about the price of notoriety.

Just as I was stepping into the CFO role in late 2007, the *Wall Street Journal* was launching a new magazine, *Portfolio*. Through our press relations department at Lehman, they had requested I do an interview with them. It was pre-cleared by the firm as an interview they would be comfortable with. I can't imagine anyone at Leman really understood how *Portfolio* was trying to position itself, as some type of glamour magazine for the Street. I really hope not. That became apparent to me later on. But I had absolutely no idea. It had danger written all over it right from the very beginning when they called my assistant to say they wanted to take pictures at a nearby luxury hotel. What was wrong with my office or a conference room? That's where I had taken previous press pictures. Photographers bring in their own lighting anyway. That seemed strange, but not nearly as strange as their other requests. They asked that I wear an evening gown. I mean really? An evening gown? I told them no way I would do that. They would have to come to our office and they could take whatever photos they wanted following the interview. All of it would take place in my regular work clothes. No special outfits. No costumes. Just me at work. Jesus, I had some boundaries.

What I should have done was immediately gone to my colleagues who managed press relations and told them I shouldn't do the interview because of the direction the magazine was headed. But I didn't. I am embarrassed to admit that I think on some level I was flattered, and that clouded my good sense. It's hard to say exactly how I felt, but maybe I was pleased that someone was seeing a real person beyond the career-driven brainiac. I had been all substance for so long that maybe a flattering veneer had some appeal. Maybe that's why Marissa Mayer of Yahoo did that *Vogue* shoot. We're still women, even as CEOs and CFOs.

In retrospect, the piece came out badly for me. It would not be the only press item to do so, but it was the first. All the press I'd had prior to that point had focused on my professional accomplishments and creativity. The *Portfolio* article, however, spent more time on my clothing choices than on my skills. The final pictures were inappropriate. They asked to shoot me getting out of a car in front of our office building and the whole thing was just obnoxious. You'd think my colleagues who worked with the press at Lehman would kept the piece in line, but the actual interview and photo shoot were not attended by anyone experienced enough to make any executive decisions about it. But it really should have been on me. Lehman had their own branding strategy and whether this fit or not was on someone else's watch. It was up to me, though, not to be a jackass.

From that point in December of 2007 through the next six months until June of 2008 when I resigned—and after—media attention became a fact of my life. And the reality of that type of exposure is that you actually start to believe, for all the wrong reasons, that you matter. That you're important. Between television, newspapers, and magazines, I was covered constantly. I thought it was great. The people around me thought it was great. If I was feeling like a rock star, part of that was that I let the people around me treat me like a rock star. That included those closest to me, who probably should have reminded me that all this attention didn't change a thing about who I really was. If I was loved or liked, it should have been for some other reason. All that success shouldn't have mattered. But I think it did. The only person who was not completely on board with Erin the Wall Street Rock Star was Anthony. Don't get me wrong, he sincerely admired and respected what I had done with my life and the hard work and talent that were required to get there. But that's it. It didn't mean more to him than that. All the other trappings of the success of my career were less important to him. Being famous on Wall Street and the financial rewards that came with it may have been interesting to him, but I was more interesting. Me. But it was still too early in our relationship for him to tell me to shut it down, that I shouldn't be so flattered. That it wasn't the real me.

The spotlight of the press ramped up dramatically in March of 2008 after the near collapse of Bear Stearns. Only a couple of days later, I had to deliver Lehman's first quarter earnings call. I believed I had to be out there, on offense. Telling "our" story. Why Lehman was different. Why we were not destined to go the same way as Bear Stearns. On June 1, the *New York Post* printed an article entitled "The 50 Most Powerful Women in NYC" and I was number three. Number three? Are you serious? I was right behind Hillary Clinton and Anna Wintour. It was ridiculous. And forget all the coverage of what came a few short weeks later in mid-June when I resigned amid a tremendous second quarter loss for Lehman and a bigger mess. Ah, how much can change in a few months. But, that's how it works. You love the attention, you hate the attention. For me, the old adage "Any press is good press" did not apply. I withered with the bad press. When I look back, it seems like much more press was probably negative than positive. Maybe it just feels that way because it hurt. An image was created of me that I had no control over.

I did one brief magazine interview after I arrived for my short stay at Credit Suisse in the fall of 2008 when I left Lehman. I did it at the request of Credit Suisse because I think they felt it was good coverage for them. That was the last of it. I completely eliminated any press after that. I wouldn't speak to the media or step out in public again in any way for almost five years. I feared anything to do with public exposure. I wanted to move on in life, to just be a regular person. To take a shot at living a more peaceful life. Maybe get married and have a child. To me, the most ordinary things were extraordinary. To be able to have a baby—which women did every day, every hour, every minute without any special skills, training, or talent—would be extraordinary. That's what began to motivate me. Looking at ordinary families living ordinary lives and recognizing there was something extraordinary in all of it. I didn't want to be on the front page of the *Wall Street Journal,* I wanted to be driving on the beach in a jeep for the afternoon for a picnic and some fishing with kids in tow. I marveled at the families that did such things and their lives. I am sure I was overstating their happiness or the perfection of the picture, but even knowing that, I was still mesmerized by it, by the idea that I could find happiness in simple things outside of my career success.

Maybe before this developing epiphany—which began in earnest in 2009, with tremendous help from Anthony—there were some people who tried to point out that my life needed a different focus or different direction. One person who I think tried to deliver a not so subtle message about my mislaid priorities was my colleague Steve Lessing. Steve sat on the Executive Committee with me and is one of those extremely charming people who exudes warmth and goodwill. As a result, he was a master salesman and had held various senior sales executive positions along the course of his long career at Lehman. In 2006–2007, Steve had been in charge of client relationship management and headed a small group of very seasoned bankers who focused solely on enhancing the relationships with some of Lehman's most profitable clients.

Steve and I had spent a lot of time together in my hedge fund job in 2007 right before I became CFO, but in 2005 and early 2006, we didn't know each other quite so well. I recall being in a car together in early 2006 with some other colleagues on the way to a visit with Met-Life, one of our insurance company clients. We were chatting about a range of topics, including religion. I was making it clear that I wasn't very religious when Steve interjected pretty forcefully, "Oh Erin, your poor father!" It struck me immediately that he saw our relationship in the vein of a father-daughter. I was too old to really be his daughter, but he did have a bit of that paternalistic approach with me. "What do you mean?" I queried, laughing because he had said it with a chuckle. For the record, I certainly felt like I'd been a very good daughter to my father and only imagined some sort of joke was in the works here. "There are three things you need to do to make your father happy," he explained. Now note, Steve had never met my father.

"Okay. Here they are. You need to play golf, become a Republican, and believe in God." Now I really laughed. Golf, conservative politics, and God? The missing pieces of my life? My father's lament was that he didn't have a daughter who cared about those things? I don't doubt now that what I took as a joke at the time he meant seriously. Tough love cloaked in humor. I am pretty sure he would have said something about having a family, meaning children, if he thought it was okay to go that far, but given that we weren't good friends yet, he probably felt he couldn't say that. That territory was fraught with danger when it came to female colleagues. So I've carried around this memory of a small story thinking it was cute and funny on a conscious level. But as I think about it now, my subconscious knew better. I deliberately kept this vignette in my memory bank to open up and reconsider at some later point in time. What was Steve really saying to me? Now I think he was saying that there was more to life than running around to client meetings to win business and trying to get fulfillment from promotions and deal mandates.

Playing golf meant take time to enjoy yourself, spending time with friends and family and being someone to have fun with. Republicanism meant caring about people in your community, being part of something that you believe in other than your next new product idea. It meant giving a shit about the bigger picture and recognizing your role in it. Then there was God. God was simple. Be spiritual. Have a soul. Have an enlightened commitment to the good you can do in the universe. Maybe I'm reading too much into a quick interaction, but I am certain it was much more seriously intended than the circumstances appeared. Even though I didn't heed his words at the time, what I feel good about is that Steve cared about me. Those were all very valid points about the nature of my existence at the time, and I see it less as criticism and more as an indication that he saw something in me that made him believe change was possible.

The idea of my potential reminds me of another story where I was traveling with colleagues a year or so prior. Brad, one of the senior guys, was ribbing my boss Larry. "Now, Larry," he said, "look at Erin. She is clearly living up to her potential. But you could be doing more," he said with laughter. Strangely, I interpreted this remark as an insult. "Maybe, I'm not living up to my potential," I squawked. Now all of this related to work and so did my response, but in an odd way, I didn't want to think I was living up to my potential. I didn't want to believe I was the best I could be. I wanted to be better. I always wanted to be better. Brad meant it as a compliment, I'm sure, but these were the crazy thoughts that went through my head.

Maybe we want people to see who we can be as much as who we actually are. I know I eventually did. That's what Anthony represents to me. He was the person, in my forty-nine years, who saw my potential better than anyone. He didn't see me as an investment banker, a lawyer, a student, or an athlete. He recognizes my achievements in all those things, but he also says very clearly that I can be better at living my life. And as I much as I hate that at times, it's what I want. Fittingly, Anthony has helped me realize at least some of Steve's suggestions about golf, Republicanism, and God. I play golf now. Yes, after all those years of resisting it, I love it. And, further, I am better at having fun now in so many ways. My natural penchant for being serious hasn't changed, but I've lightened up a lot thanks to his encouragement. I can be silly. I can let myself go. I am more fun to be around. That's better for everyone in my life. As to politics, I am no longer a registered Democrat. I actually voted for Romney in the 2012 presidential election. The important fact is that I am more open-minded and thoughtful about candidates and issues. I will consider all sides completely. I care about what community I am a part of, a notion that was foreign to me. Does it reflect my values? Do I feel at home? And as for God, having been raised as a Catholic attending Catholic schools, Anthony convinced me to go back to church in early 2009 when I was still at a low point. He thought it could help me and he was right. I did find comfort. Meaning. My belief in God and faith in a community of believers is now a consistent and important part of my life. I am often at church on Sunday when an element of one of the scriptures really strikes me. It resonates with me, and says something about my life that I need to hear. I am open to it. I am listening for it. I want to be there. I want to be better.

So somehow by 2007 I think I had fully lost my way on a variety of fronts. Even on a more mundane score, for all the improvement I'd made as a team player over the dozen years after I started at Lehman Brothers in 1995, by 2007 when I became CFO I had fallen back into an abyss of individualism and isolation. I regressed on a dozen years of progress in a few months. That was partly my own fault, partly the practical realities of the job, and partly the dynamics of the executives around me. I am so disappointed in myself for that. Even in the most basic and fundamental aspects of my job, I felt like I was back on my own. For the twelve years prior, I had insisted on sitting on a trading floor with open, attached desks where your entire team is sitting together with each teammate in your sight lines at all angles, making communication about clients, market dynamics, or last night's episode of 24 simple and easy. I loved this. I had no problem shutting out all the chatter and distractions as needed, and it was well worth the upside of sitting with my colleagues each day in an open forum.

The whole setup of the executive level was isolating. That's where Dick, the CEO, and Joe, the president, and some other members of the Executive Committee had their office, and it was important to be near them. For the first time since 1995, I had to sit in an office by myself. To put it mildly, I didn't like it at all, but the nature of my job necessitated that setup. I certainly couldn't be reviewing or discussing sensitive information about Lehman Brothers on an open trading floor, and it was important to be physically near Dick and Joe, who spoke with me several times a day. It was lonely. A few days a week I would wander downstairs to the trading floors to talk to friends and colleagues. I'd kill two birds with one stone. I was getting good current market information, which was critical to my job, and, importantly, it made me feel connected to people, part of the team. I tried to pretend that things hadn't changed so much. But they had. I was no longer talking to the head of equities or debt capital markets as Erin, because now they were talking to the CFO.

My friends and colleagues looked at me differently. They kept a safe distance. I was too important to treat the way they'd used to treat me. But I'd liked the old way. The way that I imagined allowed me to be a better version of myself.

I have spent years struggling back from losing my way, my values. In a certain light, it seems like a long journey, even though the period of my past that I am most disappointed with only lasted a year. But those forces had been building in a negative direction for so many years prior to that, and I guess it takes a while to reflect, admit, and recover.

Anthony and I were watching an HBO documentary recently called *State of Play*. The topic was happiness. The focus of the show was on highly successful NFL football players who had retired and subsequently struggled with a sense of purpose and identity following the end of their football careers. What was their identity other than as a great player? What were they good at other than football? What did their day-to-day, get up, live, and go to sleep look like without the regimen of football?

I could relate to almost every single thing about their experiences when I left Lehman in June of 2008 and subsequently left Credit Suisse the following year in 2009—that time leaving Wall Street for good. The show used a phrase that was new to me, "posttraumatic growth." The idea that after a life crisis we can change fundamentally and, sometimes, in a radically positive way. This is how I feel now; although it took more than half a decade, I have changed in a positive way. I am finally living up to my potential. I don't know if that would have happened without the personal crisis I would live through. I needed to run into a wall at a hundred miles an hour and fall down with stars circling around my head. It couldn't be subtle. It had to be brutal to break the fortress of determination I had built for myself.

But all these events and changes were still yet to come in the early months of 2008. I think about that winter and early spring the same way I think about having passed an accident on the other side of the Long Island Expressway. On your side the traffic is flowing, but on the other side it is at a dead stop. But then you get a few miles past it and see the cars on the other side still traveling in the other direction at fifty-five or sixty miles per hour. They have no idea what's ahead. That was me. Flying down the highway oblivious. No clue as to what was coming, still thinking everything would work out just fine. It really did in the big picture, but only after I was in the middle of one of the biggest pileups in recent banking history. I was headed into the collapse of Bear Stearns, then Lehman Brothers, and ultimately, a near-death experience for the entire global financial system as we knew it.

CHAPTER TWELVE

"Good Luck"

SUNDAY, MARCH 16, 2008, was no ordinary day. I was sitting in my office on Seventh Avenue in Times Square. It was pretty typical for me to work on a Sunday, but rare that I would be physically sitting in my office. It felt weird, but then again, the events of the week leading up to that day were absolutely surreal. Bear Stearns had almost collapsed a few days earlier, and would have absent a late-week purchase by J.P. Morgan. We'd learned Friday morning that the purchase price of Bear Stearns by J.P. Morgan was for two dollars per share. Two measly dollars. The stock had been at eighty dollars per share only six months prior. There was no meaningful advance warning of this calamitous event. I'd heard rumors for a few weeks prior that things weren't looking so good at Bear, but nothing substantive and nothing of this dimension, mostly ripples through the risk management team on counter-party issues. In fact, earlier in the week, Dick had prerecorded his first quarter earnings overview webcast for employees before he left on a trip for India. He wasn't even planning on being in New York for our first quarter earnings announcement in mid-March, since I was scheduled to deliver it for the first time. That's how little any of us expected what happened.

I was just trying to get my bearings. I was three months into the CFO job and this would be my first solo earnings announcement. Given that, I probably would have been in the office that Sunday in any event, only two days before my big debut. But now, layered on top of my fledgling earnings call was a looming meltdown in the capital markets, financial stocks in particular. Immediately on the heels of the Bear Stearns events, if you followed any media, the world apparently looked to Lehman as the next weak link in the banking world. We were the smallest remaining investment bank. The least diversified. The most vulnerable to a deteriorating fixed income market. The nice, run-of the-mill, straightforward earnings speech we'd been finalizing that week had to be seriously changed.

So that was one thread running through that Sunday. We had to change the speech. Make sure we made it clear what was different about Lehman from Bear Stearns. No one around me seemed to doubt that distinction as far as I could tell, it was just about communicating the message effectively. The dozens of people involved in crafting each word for the speech were trying to do just that—lawyers, accountants, investor relations employees, business units, and so on. But actually delivering the message would be my job. It was becoming clear that Sunday that the fate of Lehman Brothers might hang in the balance. If I could communicate the facts clearly and confidently, we would be fine. We had to believe that. I had to believe that. That was my mission.

Another issue on that Sunday was a vigorous debate about whether to move up our earnings call a day from Tuesday morning to Monday morning. Monday was the next day. Some members of the Executive

Committee didn't want to give the markets a full business day to impact our stock price while investors guessed about Lehman's performance for the quarter. We could try to give them the information ahead of the US market opening the next day. In retrospect, thank goodness we had that weekend to work on all those things without market activity. We needed every last second of that weekend. Like everything else, moving the earnings call was not a simple decision. If we announced on that Sunday that we were moving the call up to Monday, the market might perceive that we were trying to get bad news out there, not good news, and Asia and Europe could cause chaos before the US market ever opened. We decided to reconvene at 5 a.m. on Monday, at the office, after the Asian markets had opened, to make a final decision on the earning's call. Maybe Monday, maybe Tuesday. It was hard for me to have a strong opinion on any of this. Ninety days as CFO didn't qualify me as an expert on these kinds of decisions. I just had to be ready.

Top to bottom, it was really a shit storm when you think about it. I can barely remember what I was really feeling on that March 16. My guess is I wasn't feeling much of anything. What could I feel? It wasn't exactly what I thought I had signed up for when I said yes to the job a year earlier, but that's life. What we expect may bear little resemblance to the outcome. It's more about how you handle the unexpected. It's not like I could share all these issues with anyone. Almost all of it was confidential information. I remember leaving the office that Sunday evening with what seemed like a dozen balls in the air and meeting Anthony at a restaurant on the Upper West Side for a few hours. It was his cousin's thirtieth birthday and they'd been celebrating since the afternoon. I was glad he was busy. When I got there,

I had a beer and hung out for a little while before we headed for dinner and home. I couldn't say a word.

Anthony was marching with the FDNY in the St. Patrick's Day parade in Manhattan the next day, and he'd asked if I'd be able to sneak out for an hour to see him go down Fifth Avenue. He'd be wearing his "dress blues" and proudly walking side by side with his colleagues. That possibility was completely implausible, but he had no idea. I barely knew what tomorrow would bring, but I knew I had to get to bed early enough to be up at 4 a.m. to start the next chapter. As it turns out, it was the last time Anthony would march in the parade. He still could I guess, as a retired firefighter, but it was the last time he would march with his friends and comrades as an active duty New York City firefighter. I am sad I missed that. I truly regret it. For what end? Did I save Lehman? Did it change anything?

The seventeenth of March is almost impossible to recall. No good memories. No real memory at all other than of sitting in a big conference room of people reviewing the earnings speech, since that morning the decision had been made to keep the call on Tuesday. All I know is that by the end of the day, Lehman's stock price had dropped more than 40 percent. And the next day, on March 18, it would be my job to deliver the news of Lehman's earnings. Stop the bleeding. Heal the patient. An endless array of metaphors come to mind.

Just before eight o'clock that Tuesday morning, I reread the final version of the earnings speech that dozens and dozens of people had labored over for weeks. The speech had even been feverishly reworked over the last two days on the heels of the Bear collapse. At just about eight, I walked down the hall to attend Dick's presentation to senior members of the firm. Dick had flown back from India almost as soon as he had landed. It would be impossible for him to be out of the office given what had transpired. Dick was the CEO. He talked through the numbers and outlook to the small group of fifty senior employees. The quarter looked decent and some of the panic that had been setting in for the prior few days seemed alleviated. But this crowd was composed of the believers, or at least those who wanted to and needed to believe. In a little more than an hour, I had to face the realists and the skeptics. The unbelievers. It certainly wasn't clear that convincing them would be possible. Dick then walked past my table, patted me on the back, and said, "Good luck." That's it. Good luck. The biggest financial crisis in his forty years in the business, and the viability of Lehman in the balance. Well, what did I really expect? Some detailed road map for Crisis Management 101? "Good luck" about summed it up.

I went back to my office for a short while, and then at about 9:45 a.m., I made my way to a small conference room with three young men who worked for me. We were as unimposing as you could imagine. There was no caped crusader among us. Just the four of us to face not only a rising tide against us, but a full-blown tsunami. I knew what we needed to accomplish, but I had never done this before. Although typically in my career up to that point I relished the "first" of anything, this was a horse of a different color. It was hard to muster that type of bravado, nor would it have been appropriate. We dialed into the conference call and the operator told us that there were more than ten thousand people on the line and we had to wait because so many more were trying to get on the call. I yearned to shut the whole thing down. We have enough people, for God's sake! But everyone deserved to hear me directly and have the chance to ask questions. The idea that my voice and my words were so important to these multitudes was mind-boggling. It didn't feel powerful. It felt scary. I was nervous, trust me, and I don't really ever get nervous.

I know this story may be hard to believe. It is me and I remember it well and it is still hard to believe. How could I have thought I could handle my first earnings call in the midst of such a crisis with no prior experience and no other management participation? I was told at the time that although Dick's participation had been considered, the decision was that he shouldn't be on the call. It might spook investors for him to be present, since he had never been on an earnings call before. It was never mentioned, that I remember, that Joe might participate. In any event, I didn't have a vote in these decisions. I accepted the collective wisdom and I bought their predicted version of events. At the time, all I could think was that if they had that much confidence in me that I could handle it on my own, they must be right. It really was not a good decision and that seems so obvious. Of course the CEO should be on an earnings call in the midst of an industry-wide and company-specific crisis. He was the captain of the ship, wasn't he? There was no pretending that life was business as usual. I don't believe it would have spooked anyone if Dick had been on the call. Maybe, just maybe, Dick's presence might have given a better sense that there was a capable hand on the tiller.

Despite what I strongly believe now was, at a minimum, a flawed strategy about how to handle the situation, the call itself went well, the stock rallied, and Lehman went on to live another day. So, did it really matter in the scheme of things that it was basically me doing the call on my own? It turned out to matter a lot, more than I ever could have predicted at the time. Since I was the sole presenter on the call, every public statement about Lehman that was part of the speech and the Q&A is totally attributed to me. Just me. As if I invented the information in the recesses of my brain for the hell of it. As if a whole team had not worked together to craft every word. From what I understand in all the litigation and investigations I have been involved in over the last four years, I have heard secondhand that Dick and Joe have both suggested they don't remember reading the earnings speech prior to the conference call. They have also suggested they don't remember actually listening to the call. Maybe something got lost in translation as this information filtered back to me in the legal process. But if that's true, I must admit, it blows my mind. It's not like it was a big deal, right? Why would they bother listening to the earnings call? Maybe they had something better to do.

It troubles me even today that I didn't say no. I should have insisted that Dick or Joe be on the call. Two things were going on here. First, I was convinced they cared about me and wouldn't put me in a position to fail so quickly. Think about it for a second. Most of Dick's and Joe's net worth was tied up in Lehman Brothers. My success on March 18 was critical to them. To me, that blows any conspiracy theory out of the water, or at least undermines the concept that I was set up to fail. Granted, it doesn't change the fact that they were able to distance themselves from the information given on the call. Second, I have to think that hubris had a hand in my willingness to go along with the plan. I believed in myself and my capabilities, perhaps to a fault. I thought I could handle it. I believed it was possible for me to pull this off. As the markets continued to suffer and Lehman contended with those risks, what I failed to appreciate was that my colleagues had begun to look out for themselves. That's human nature. It's just surprising that I didn't get it and start to look out for myself. After that day, Anthony told me about the way rookie firefighters in their first-year probationary period, known as "probies," are handled in the FDNY. He said that a senior firefighter would never let a probie go into a burning building first and certainly not alone. Well, looked at in this light, the March earnings call was my first burning building. I definitely qualified as a probie. And Lehman wasn't the FDNY, unfortunately. It was every man for himself.

Despite what seemed like a pull back from the brink of disaster in March 2008, we all know that would not ultimately be a positive turning point for Lehman Brothers. And though I looked like the company hero in mid-March, I would ignominiously tumble off my lofty perch in less than three months' time. But during those few months of free fall, life still went on. As my colleagues and I used to say to each other before we had a meeting with an important, imposing client, "He still puts his pants on one leg at a time." So did I. I still had to get up in the morning and go to work as if what was happening was normal. We're still just human beings trying to do our best, making mistakes. We aren't characters in a movie. This was my life, not some miniseries melodrama, even though it had all the right attributes for a good show. I have recited the details of this time endlessly in investigations and litigation as it relates to the CFO job, and my life outside of work was a continuing struggle despite the presence of Anthony.

I remember being constantly exhausted in those few months after the mid-March earnings. I was still functioning at a high level, but I was like a little kid up past her bedtime, excited and active and you couldn't get me to sleep. I know my mother often used to call my sisters and I "overtired" when we were young. I was running on some version of anxiety and adrenaline at a hyper pace, but I was truly tired. One Saturday in May, I had been up early working out and following up on some work-related issues, and I fell asleep in the middle of the day. This was not at all unusual for me on a Saturday afternoon. I think Saturday afternoons were the only time I felt I was truly allowed to take a break because Sundays had to be focused on getting ready for Monday again. And while I was asleep, Anthony left me in the East Hampton house and took the half-hour drive out to Montauk for the night where some friends and family had gathered.

Anthony was not my ex-husband Michael. He was not going to sit around enabling me to let this all-encompassing job dominate both of our lives. If Saturday afternoon was part of the little bit of quality time we got to spend together each week and I chose to sleep through it, he wasn't going to put up with it. I couldn't even blame my behavior on the crisis situation because Saturday naps had been part of my repertoire for a couple of years. I used them to recharge my battery. Recharge it for work, not for life. As much as I loved Anthony and wanted him in my life, I still thought I could stay the course on giving a half-assed version of myself to the people I cared about. I remember feeling upset at the time that he had left, but I didn't decide that I needed some fundamental change in my own behavior. Not yet.

What else stands out from those last few months as CFO as things got further and further away from me? I don't want to bore you with the Lehman details. Or rather, maybe they are best left for another story. Others have written stories about those events, all of the actions and decisions of those last few months. But that is not the story I care to tell. I did have my struggles at work in that period that were not just about the financial state of Lehman Brothers. Some of those difficulties were exacerbated as a woman in a man's world. At one point, Dick had a conversation with me where he told me that he felt I had a tendency to be too hard on the other, all-male, members of the Executive Committee. My interrogatory style could be off-putting and challenging. It was definitely my modus operandi to ask a lot of questions. It always had been. I had that reputation throughout my career. From my perspective, I felt my questions were always intended to get at a better understand on a point, and really shouldn't have felt threatening. Obviously, that's not how everyone saw it. Someone must have complained to Dick that I asked too many questions, or they didn't like the way I asked them. It was ironic to be told to ease up a little by Dick and his tough-guy persona. And who knows. Just as I had managed to become even more intense and extreme year after year, maybe I had lost some of my diplomatic touch.

Of course at the time I found it a bit laughable that these dozen men with all their hundreds of years of collective experience thought I was being tough on them. I really wasn't a hard-ass or rude, but I was direct and persistent. I can't help but think my being a woman played a part in the committee's reaction. I am not trying to shirk my responsibility for my behavior, but I think it may have been particularly unexpected when you looked at me. Not that anyone anticipated I would be some shrinking violet, but I may not have looked the part of Hulk Hogan. In fairness, this was new territory for of all of us, and maybe less so for me than for my male colleagues. This wasn't the first time I had been the only woman in a meeting, on a committee, or in a whole host of circumstances, but it was the most significant scenario where that was the case. So as much as I may have thought it wasn't that big a deal, it was a big deal. My presence in the room wasn't going to become normal overnight. It would take some time. I did try to take Dick's feedback to heart, however, and pay closer attention to how I asked my questions. I didn't stop asking them, though.

In these same few months, Joe called me into his office one afternoon and sat me down across from him at his conference table. I figured it would be a serious conversation, since he closed the door and wasn't sitting at his desk. His actions all seemed quite deliberate. And presumably they were as he started to delve into what was obviously a sensitive topic. He wanted to discuss my clothing. Since, as he put it, I was the only person in the room during an Executive Committee meeting whose legs are showing, it created a unique situation. He went on to tell me that some of my clothes were too provocative. So much so that he felt that some of my colleagues were distracted during meetings because of what I was wearing. That's what happens I guess when you have all men around the table for so long. I won't name names, but he did. I couldn't have been more surprised. I had certainly developed a more feminine style of dress over the few years prior to that, after having spent so many years in pantsuits. I felt able to do that as I had become more confident in my success, and I no longer felt I had to conform to the notion of a sexless, tasteless female executive. The idea that my appearance was inappropriate was surprising. I really didn't know how to respond. I made adjustments because now I felt self-conscious. Every morning that I got up and dressed for work after that conversation, I thought hard about whether my clothes were too revealing, too sexy. Distracting? Here I am in the middle of a market meltdown and trying to keep my head above water and I am worried about my clothes? It seems stupid, but I wanted to do everything in my power to do my job well. If a clothing adjustment was part of it, so be it.

So being a woman had its moments and its unique considerations. I think most of the time I was oblivious to the distinction, but that didn't mean others were. I still feel very strongly, though, that—as with everything in life—you take the good with the bad. The uniqueness of my gender cut both ways, and on balance, I always saw it as a positive. No one tended to forget me. I didn't fade into the sea of dark suits that my clients would meet year after year to pitch them business. I wasn't trying to be one of the guys. The fact that I had gained confidence to bring the real me to the office by the time I was CFO at Lehman was a big evolution from my early days as a lawyer at Simpson Thacher & Bartlett as the disembodied intellect. I think those who worked with me closely at Lehman in those last few years felt they really knew me as a person and knew what was going on with me. That worked for me. If I was going to live my entire life in those four walls of 745 Seventh Avenue, I might as well do it as the real me, however one-dimensional she had become.

By mid-May of 2008, a certain set of events involving David Einhorn took a personal turn in a way that will always seem bizarre to me. For those of you who are unfamiliar with David, he is a hedge fund investor of some public renown. In late 2007 and early 2008, Lehman was in his sights and he was on the record regarding issues he had with the firm. Believe it or not, there is not a lot to tell about my interaction with David Einhorn. He requested a call in May of 2008 to review some questions. Typically, at that time, companies would ignore these types of requests. But, again, in the collective wisdom of Lehman management, I was told I should do the call with him. Easy for them to say, right? There was no conceivable upside and tremendous downside. It's not like I thought I would change his mind. I wasn't that arrogant. But there was a view that we should take on all naysayers at that point. Not hide from them. So I took the call with two young men who worked for me. Although not a very long call, it did not go well. The tone was definitely antagonistic, and by the following week he was speaking at a conference to announce his short in Lehman's stock.

The call was clearly another bad decision, but what was truly weird to me, though, was how it was handled in the press. It was presented as a battle between me and Einhorn. Not me, as the CFO of Lehman, who was speaking to him on behalf of the company, but me Erin Callan. A *New York Times* story on the front page of the business section in early June depicted a boxing match marquee with both our pictures. "David Einhorn vs. Erin Callan" was the headline. I never understood why it became a personal battle. We never spoke again after that phone call in mid-May. I have never even met him in person. The two of us had no history to speak of. Maybe it just made it a more interesting media story to cast it in this light. That's the only explanation I have.

The idea that David Einhorn and I were engaged in some personal, mortal combat was not unique to the *New York Times*. I remember getting ready for work one morning in early June. I was stepping out of the shower and I had CNBC playing on my television, half-listening to the morning business news stories. "Well, I think she is more likable than he is," the anchor was saying. I turned to look at the screen and there were our two pictures once again. The topic of conversation was the battle between us and who was more likable. It was surreal, these two people talking about me like that. What the hell? What was going on? I truly felt I had lost all sense of control over myself and how I was portrayed. Our one conversation had snowballed into a complete disaster of unforeseen consequences. And now I was paying the price in the media for decisions I wasn't making.

The Einhorn call and its aftermath became such a distraction to the firm in my mind that in the days that followed I went to Joe to suggest for the first time that I resign as CFO. It wasn't easy to say that to him, nor did I really want to, but I expressed my concern about the fallout of the Einhorn situation and how I had seemed to become the lightning rod for Lehman criticism as the only public face of the company. The idea of resigning, which seemed like a complete capitulation and recognition of failure in the role, was very hard for me to handle. So although I suggested it to Joe and I meant it, I didn't demand it.

With the Einhorn fiasco still very much alive and kicking, the really bad news in early June of 2008 was that it was apparent Lehman was going to have a large loss for the second quarter. The critics and skeptics would be vindicated, and it seemed bad. Mid-May to mid-June just felt like the slow buildup of a twister that was headed in my direction. I started to see it on the horizon and still thought it was possible to get to a safe place. To hunker down. I still wanted to stay the course. I still thought it was possible, but I was running out of time.

Lehman Brother's second quarter closed on May 31, and the earnings call was slated for a few weeks after. The announcement of a large loss was now officially looming as the numbers got finalized. In today's world, the ability to keep that type of blockbuster information quiet for a few weeks was virtually impossible. So this time, unlike March, it was decided the earnings call should be moved up a week. Hopefully we could prevent the bad information from leaking out early, when there was no ability to control the story. Some good things had happened in the quarter, or at least we had some facts that could cushion the blow of the loss a bit and indicate that Lehman had decided to act more drastically to right the ship. We hoped the good things would matter. If you had followed a chart of our share price, there was a low in March, just before the earnings call, that bounced back up on that day. But the line again began a slow descent downward thereafter. There was still plenty of room at the bottom of the chart. The June earnings announcement didn't create the bounce we hoped for. It went over like a lead balloon.

Strange to be at the center of all these dramatic events as a relative newcomer. It is so easy to see in the aftermath how significant Lehman's second quarter loss would turn out to be, and what effect that would have on the firm's viability and that Lehman would no longer exist as a going concern. But at the time, on June 8, 2008, I didn't think in terms like that. I had no real sense of the macro-level effects and was completely clueless about what any of it meant for me personally. It all felt very random that I was in that place at that time. Not fateful. Not predestined. Just pure randomness. That made it harder to deal with all the fallout later on. I never considered somehow this was "meant to be" for me. What it really felt like was "shit happens." That says it all.

CHAPTER THIRTEEN

Shell-Shocked

THIRTEEN HAS ALWAYS been my lucky number. I know it's contrary and I don't have a good explanation for it. It just is. Ironically, it is Anthony's lucky number, too. True soul mates, huh? Still, June 13, 2008, didn't feel so lucky. That was the day after I resigned my job as chief financial officer of what was Lehman Brothers in a spectacularly public humiliation. I say "was" because, a few months after, Lehman Brothers would no longer be an operating business. After 158 years, it disappeared in a cataclysmic meltdown that seemed to take the global economy with it. To add insult to injury, that June 13 was Friday the thirteenth. I guess I should have known it wouldn't be a good day. My head was killing me and I was disoriented. I was in my bed in my house in East Hampton. On a weekday? Why wasn't I in the city? Why was I still asleep on a day that I typically would have already been up, exercised, and fully kicked into high gear at work? Panic struck me. I would be so late getting to work. What meetings was I missing? I needed to call my assistant and let her know. And then it hit me. No one was waiting for me. I didn't have any meetings.

I technically didn't even really have a job, although I was still an employee at Lehman Brothers. Everything had changed.

Thursday, June 12, 2008, felt like a surrealistic nightmare. I woke up at my regular time of 5:30 a.m. I didn't work out that day, which was unusual, but the night before I knew it would be a rough sleep and I had a good reason to skip my exercise. I managed to hold it together while I took a shower and got dressed. I had no idea what I was wearing that day, which is very weird for me. I was almost unconscious going through my morning routine to get ready for work. Uncharacteristically, I grabbed a pair of sunglasses as I walked out the door of my apartment, a good move because they came in very handy as I walked out the front door of the Lehman Brothers offices at 745 Seventh Avenue in Manhattan several hours later. Anthony, my husband, drove me to work that morning as he had started to do that last month. I was working more and more hours and things were getting more complicated. Getting a ride with him made it a little more bearable.

On June 12, the car ride with Anthony was a pleasant respite for a few minutes, just the two of us, before I stepped into mayhem. He dropped me across the street from the office on West Forty-Eighth Street so I could make my mandatory stop at Dunkin' Donuts for coffee. I would really need it that morning. I wasn't tired but my energy was low. I walked in the side entrance of the Lehman building. In the middle of Times Square, the building always looked active at any time of day or night due to the bright signage that was mandatory for buildings in the area. Even with the frenetic flavor of those streets, more was happening inside than anyone imagined.

A 7:30 a.m. meeting of the Executive Committee of Lehman was scheduled. The thirteen-person—twelve men, one woman—

committee that was responsible for running the firm had important business. I rode the elevator to the thirty-first floor, as I'd been doing for the past eight months. I walked in my office and looked around and didn't know where to begin. I couldn't think. Of course there were a million things I should have done. I should have organized all my personal stuff, pictures, letters, files. I lived my life at work and everything important in every part of my life was in my office. I would never get most of it back.

I am sure everything from my office is labeled and boxed somewhere and has been looked at by hundreds of lawyers, paralegals, and investigators. You could really piece together a tremendous amount about my life from what was in my office. I miss the letters the most. There were letters that came to me at work. Just publishing those letters would have been a cool book. You'd be amazed how many people still write letters, and over the years, I got letters from clients and colleagues that made me realize the personal impact you can have in your career. I had crazy letters, too—you'd be shocked how many convicted felons are actively watching CNBC. Letters from people I'd met over the course of my entire life. As a kid. As a young adult. Who wanted to say something and did so eloquently and thoughtfully. I miss those letters. They would have helped me remember more of what was good when all I could see for a long time in the aftermath was what went wrong and how I let it crush me.

In any event, I don't remember doing anything when I came into my office other than sitting at my desk, sipping some coffee, and waiting for the meeting. As it got closer to 7:30 a.m., my fellow Executive Committee members began to file past my office toward the conference room. It was next to my office so they could not avoid me. But, trust me, no one looked at me. They couldn't make eye contact. You'd think I'd be the one who couldn't look up from my desk, but it was the other way around. I was "dead man walking." No one wanted to go near me. I didn't want to go in there, though, until I thought everyone was seated. There was absolutely no way I was going to sit in there and make small talk until Dick showed up. When it seemed everyone was likely there, I walked in and took my regular seat by the window in the middle of the table. In the middle of the action, as I always thought. The perfect spot to be engaged and relevant, or that was the idea.

Dick came in and sat down next to me. He started talking right away, announcing that Joe Gregory and I were resigning from our respective roles. And the scene blurs, like the fade-out in a movie. I know I started to cry. I wasn't outright bawling, just quiet tears down my face. I *really* did not want to cry. So stereotypical. I never cried about anything. But that was when it hit me. I was no longer the chief financial officer of Lehman Brothers. It was the first time in my almost twenty years of working that I felt like I was taking a giant step backward. More than that, it was like stepping off a cliff. A glass cliff of sorts. I tumbled down. I had known since the previous afternoon what was happening, but now it was real. Whatever happened after that I have no idea. I think there was some discussion about next steps. Hey, but look at the bright side. At least I wouldn't have to be on the front lines facing the firing squad anymore. There was that.

Somehow, the worst meeting of my life ended and I walked the ten feet back to my office. One or two people came in to acknowledge they were sorry about what had happened. Everyone was very brief and then they were gone. Now what? What was I supposed to do next? There was no real discussion about a next job. I remember there was some reference in a proposed press release that I would take a "senior role" in investment banking, but no one had discussed that with me. There was no plan for me that I could see. Things would continue to hurtle forward in the pell-mell way they had been, and I was just some collateral damage left behind. No one had the time or inclination to think about it. As all these thoughts were beginning to take shape in my head. I heard my name. There was no one else in my office, but the constantly streaming CNBC was on in the background as usual on my desk. And there I was. My picture anyway. Charlie Gasparino had the scoop that Joe Gregory and I had been fired. A blockbuster story. Good for Charlie. It was on the news just a few minutes after the Executive Committee meeting ended. It's funny how things get deliberately leaked to the media on cue, and always with a distinct spin.

But I wasn't fired, was I? That wasn't how I understood it. I had offered to resign weeks before in the midst of the Einhorn mess because I had a pretty strong feeling I no longer had any public market confidence. The firm was struggling and I figured I had to be the one to take the fall. Easier said than done was a gross understatement. I had become the face of Lehman Brothers by design. And, perhaps by design, I had to sacrifice myself for years of decisions by others that had led to this place in this market. Dick and Joe had refused my proposed resignation a few weeks prior, but those next two weeks in late May and early June had changed everything. After the announcement of the first quarterly loss ever in Lehman's more than 150-year history, all bets were off and the circumstances begged for dramatic change. Even with new capital in hand, the markets reacted negatively. Boy, that's saying it as calmly as I can. It was really bad.

Two days earlier, on the afternoon of June 10, following a morning Executive Committee meeting, I had approached Dick again about resigning. There was no need to go to Joe first now. Dick was the CEO. He needed to know. When he didn't accept my resignation, I wrote him an e-mail that afternoon reiterating why I thought it was necessary. I have seen that e-mail and his response many times now in the litigation process. I told him I was willing to take accountability among senior management because I thought I had lost my credibility. He said no. I went home to Anthony that night and told him I felt I needed to resign and the probabilities were increasing that it would have to occur. I had started to see it as an eventuality. He was the first person I said it out loud to, besides Dick and Joe, and I barely got the words past my lips without them trembling. I remember Anthony said he would cook dinner and he went out for a half hour to the supermarket and left me limp and depressed on the couch. I couldn't imagine going anywhere. He took care of me that night, as he has always done throughout our relationship. I needed to be taken care of. I needed someone else to take charge.

I went to Dick again the next morning to discuss my resignation again. The pressure to do so in my own head was getting unbearable. He still wasn't in that place. Not yet. Later that afternoon of June 11, Joe summoned me out of a conference room full of people. We went to his office and that's when he told me. We were going to resign together. When the demands for meaningful change became too great, our resignations were the path out back to public market confidence. As president, Joe was a significant figure internally at the firm. I was well-known outside the firm. All constituents could be mollified and Lehman could move on and thrive, or that was the idea. Despite my prior resignation attempts, I was still shell-shocked. The worst part was I had to go back to the conference room of people waiting for me and act like everything was normal and continue working. I had to pull off that charade until the following morning of June 12 when a press release about our resignations would be issued.

I don't remember much detail about that meeting with Joe because I think there wasn't much to it. He didn't have much to say because he was going through his own crisis. Since he'd had the largest hand in picking me for the job, he seemed to feel some sense of responsibility for this outcome. He was emotional. I was numb. After that meeting with Joe I never spent any time with him again. Our relationship effectively was over. Each of us would go our separate ways and live our lives. I've never seen him or spoken to him again, other than quickly that next morning. It was very different with Dick. Dick didn't let it go so easily. Dick tried much harder. After the final discussion with Joe, I had to go back into the conference room and fake it. I had to keep going as if it were all business as usual. As usual as could be expected under the circumstances.

You may wonder why Joe told me we would both be resigning and I didn't hear about it from Dick first. I don't know why. But I was asked to go to Dick's office later that evening. When I walked in, he was sitting in a sort of anteroom area of his office that he never sat in. It had two armchairs and I'm guessing it was saved for these sorts of difficult conversations. It certainly had privacy. Nobody could see you. I felt like I was disappearing anyway. His overall message was about how sorry he was for what was happening. I believed everything he said. Maybe that's why what happened the next morning was such a shock to the system. I thought that through all of the challenges, I wasn't wrong. The people I trusted deserved to be trusted. They cared about me and what happened to me. Somehow we'd get past the pain of the next few days and move on. I am not suggesting he didn't mean what he was saying at the time. But his sentiment didn't quite square with what happened after.

Fast-forward to the next morning of June 12 after the Executive Committee meeting. Why was Charlie Gasparino saying I was "canned" by Dick? I had an immediate suspicion. As with most everything that went on at Lehman, I thought the idea was to make Dick look good. True or false, it felt like a very good educated guess to me. Now was the moment he needed to show strength by firing his close friend of decades, Joe, and his supposed protégée, me. Accepting a resignation just didn't have the same ring to it. We needed to be fired! I am as sure of this analysis as I am of anything. I don't know if Dick knew this was how it would be portrayed. He had so many handlers watching his back at every turn it's impossible to tell. To me it was a distinction with an earth-shattering difference. Joe was getting ready to retire in the next few years anyway, but I was forty-two years old. I was in the height of my career. How it was portrayed mattered tremendously.

All I felt capable of doing after hearing on national television that I had been fired was to call Anthony, let him know that I needed him to come get me, put on my sunglasses, grab my bag, and leave the building. Maybe ten minutes had passed since the CNBC "Breaking News". I was stunned and felt completely betrayed. If they had reported my actual resignation and made some attempt to look like they had a job for me that sounded substantial, I would have stayed there for the rest of my working days. If you pay attention to what happens when senior executives are taken out of positions, which is reported almost daily in the *Wall Street Journal*, they always get a new role that sounds important and real even if everyone who works there knows it may not be. They didn't even bother to make something up for me. I'd given Lehman every ounce of myself for thirteen years: all my focus, energy, and passion. I'd sacrificed any possible version of a personal life. The events of that morning completely rattled and devastated me. So how could I stay?

Between the short walk to the elevator and the ride to the lobby, I was starting to completely lose it. I was so thankful for the sunglasses. At least I wanted to get out the front door with some dignity. I still didn't realize I would never walk back in again to work there. I just knew at that moment I had to get out of there and far away. At the same time as I was breaking down, my phone was ringing off the hook. When I finally listened to messages in the next few days, there was an influx of calls from so many directions it was hard to process. Hedge fund clients called to commiserate and offer job opportunities; headhunters working for other big banks wanted to hire me; Jonathan Wald, who had a senior role at CNBC at the time, talked about a recurring television role or show on CNBC; two agents from William Morris left a message about watching me for several months with real interest and wanting to meet me about TV and book opportunities; Congressman Rahm Emmanuel; lent his support and told me "Don't let it get to you"; someone from the New York Yankees gave the same message. And it went on and on with a consistent theme: "You're great, don't let it get to you...and, by the way, we're interested."

I wish I could have processed all those messages and thoughts at the time. None of it really penetrated. I just was not functioning with real consciousness and perspective on the situation. I wasn't dying of cancer. I had left my job. But I felt like I had just been told that I was dying of cancer. I was full of disoriented and hopeless feelings that really were completely out of whack in retrospect. Work for me was the center of self-fulfillment and self-realization. Work was my chief source of identity. My foundation. When the bottom fell out, there wasn't enough below it to sustain me.

Until a few years ago, it still felt very difficult to talk about the events at the very end of my time at Lehman. Through the years of litigation, I would hold it together pretty well, but always stumbled a bit recounting those last few days. How was that possible after all that time? How could I still have been so emotional about these events for years later? Why couldn't I just reflect on it without distress? Now, as I have moved past that type of reaction, I see my life for what it truly is. I have a husband whom I love and who loves me, a caring family, and a wonderful life. Most precious of all is our beautiful baby girl, Maggie, the fulfillment of our hopes and dreams for the last five years. I have so much more than anyone could want. But why did it take so long to see the simplest of things? I think I do know why. For me, being happy takes discipline.

In 2005, as part of one of Lehman's management training programs, I took a test called "Authentic Happiness." The test ranks your "signature strengths" as they relate to happiness. Not surprisingly, my top signature strength was "industry, diligence, and perseverance. You work hard to finish what you start. No matter the project, you 'get it out the door' in a timely fashion. You do not get distracted when you work, and you take satisfaction in completing tasks." Boy, that was an accurate test. Anthony will laugh hard when I show him this. I am the master of execution in his eyes. Sometimes I get so focused on accomplishing something, I don't evaluate if the task even makes sense. My to-do list never ends. But is the order right? Or should some of these things even get done? He knows I can be guilty of execution for execution's sake.

My other strengths, which followed, seem a little more attractive: "Curiosity and interest in the world," "Judgment, critical thinking, and open-mindedness," and "Zest, enthusiasm and energy." But what is more interesting to me is the twenty-fourth strength, last on the list. "Appreciation of beauty and excellence. You notice and appreciate beauty, excellence and/or skilled performance *in all domains of life*, from nature to art to mathematics to science to *everyday experience*." That's is absolutely something I failed at for many years. I've tried hard to change, and I am so much better at it. Life is beautiful, if only I stop and smell the roses. See what I have, not what I don't have, not what I used to have. Everything to do with my career would get jumbled up with these feelings for so many years. Most of the time, I can now see all those years working for what they were: a time of my life with different priorities and goals, but which is still part of who I am today. I see where I am now as a new chapter with a different type of fulfillment. I expect this chapter to be more solid and lasting. Less fragile. That's what I feel and continue to strive for. The ordinary is extraordinary when looked at from the right angle, with the right mind-set. I just want number twenty-four to move up the list a bit. It has.

In any event, when I walked out into Times Square in the middle of a bright sunny morning in mid-June of 2008, I wasn't the high-functioning person I was used to. Anthony was there to help. We have done that for each other many times over these past eight years. We also picked up my sister, Beth, who left work that day for added support. We drove straight toward the East End of Long Island, making our getaway, so to speak. We stopped for lunch at a restaurant named Oakland's on the water in Hampton Bays and sat outside. I felt much more like drinking than eating. I don't think we really managed to appreciate the beautiful day as we looked out toward the beach and Atlantic Ocean. I know I didn't.

By the time we got to my house in East Hampton I had worn myself out in body and mind, and I lay down to rest for a while. Even as I did, the home telephone was ringing off the hook. No one ever called that number. No one even knew that number. It was there basically for faxing for work. It was funny to even hear it ring. There was no way I was answering that phone, nor did I care what could possibly be said from the other end of the line. Beth answered it several times. I will forever tease her about her public relations skills as a result. One of the calls that afternoon was from a *New York Times* reporter. In the next day's paper about the events of that day and their attempt to get in touch with me, the *Times* read, "Her sister said Ms. Callan was napping and could not come to the phone." Sounds super cool and casual. I was just nappin' in the middle of the day. No big deal. Why not enjoy an afternoon off? At least that's how I thought it came across. At least it didn't say that I had worn myself out from devastating humiliation through extreme emotion and crying. I tried to tell myself that it didn't matter what anyone thought anymore. I wish I was convinced of that.

I was lost. Completely lost. Untethered from my foundation of myself. If I wasn't working, I had no apparent purpose. Even with the tremendous importance of Anthony in my life at that point, I still didn't see my relationship with him as my main purpose. That would come later. It was the sudden end to twenty years of my life. But how did I get to such a crazy place about my job? It definitely hadn't only happened in those last six months as CFO. It had been building slowly and surely in that direction for twenty years. A commitment to a principle that builds that slowly is likely incredibly strong. For those first few days, I walked around like a zombie and tried to ignore newspapers and financial television. I remember going to a local place in East Hampton in the morning for some donuts and coffee, and seeing my picture on one of the newspaper front pages, I was overwhelmed with embarrassment. I just wanted to disappear. How could all that hard work and energy and sacrifice have led to this? I felt disgraced. I stayed in my hypnotic state through the weekend. Comatose Erin, at least that version of comatose, didn't last very long. By Monday morning, June 16, I had bought a new notebook. I am looking at it right now. The first page is date June 16/17 and is a meticulous list of all the phone calls I received about job opportunities over those few days, annotated with detailed notes. Next is another list of appointments for meetings and conference calls to follow up on everything that seemed worthwhile to me.

All this now seems ridiculous. The drama. Oh the drama! Was I the first person to resign, get fired, or any other version of what happened in this scenario? It is embarrassing. Embarrassing that I thought this was life or death. The crying, the meltdown, the complete lack of any perspective. I mean, really? Could anything have matched the downright havoc I let this situation wreak on me? If I had only been a little more measured in my reaction, I don't think I would have seen the next possible steps as so black and white. I know Anthony felt for me in my distress, but he didn't see any of it as catastrophic. He had seen real catastrophe in his life and this wasn't it. Far from it. So he gave better advice when I tried to figure out my next move. Stay calm. Don't rush. I didn't listen.

CHAPTER FOURTEEN

Back in the Saddle

AFTER JUNE 12, 2008, I could have decided to take a break for the first time in twenty years. I could have reflected on what had happened and how I had gotten to a place where I had made work the center of my life and then it had crushed me. Maybe I could have seriously considered if it was time to make some major changes to my existence so that I wouldn't continue down a path that seemed destined for disappointment and a lack of fulfillment. Instead, I chose to see what happened in those last few months at Lehman as a mere bump in the road in the general upward trajectory of my career. I wanted to get back in the saddle. I could salvage my damaged self-esteem by letting a whole host of other employers convince me how special I was and that they needed me desperately and immediately. That choice seemed a hell of a lot easier than the other. I wanted redemption. To prove that I was still worthy, still the talented, skilled, hard worker I believed myself to be. I wanted back in.

But even if my conscious mind wanted to jump back in with two feet, I suspect my subconscious was not fully on board. In that first week after leaving the Lehman CFO job, I started to narrow the employment choices to what I thought were the best opportunities, one of which included the hedge fund Renaissance Technologies. If you work in finance you know that Renaissance is considered by many to be the most successful hedge fund of all time. Their investment performance is unmatched. Renaissance's founder and CEO at the time, Jim Simons, frequently referred to as the "Quant King," is on the Forbes Top 100 wealthiest people in the world list with more than $10 billion of net worth. He is a brilliant mathematician and the ultimate self-made man, undeniably one of the most respected men in finance and investing. Simply put, he was "the man." Very fortunately, I had come to know Jim well between 2006 and 2008 when I did advisory work with Renaissance as an investment banker at Lehman. We had developed such a great working relationship that as soon as Renaissance found out I had left my CFO job, they called immediately.

Up to that point, most of Renaissance's investment success had been for the benefit of their few hundred employees and a handful of Jim's close friends. Their principal investment fund, called "Medallion," had, in certain years, earned close to 100 percent returns. Their investment strategy was based on mathematical models, and many employees were PhDs. The Renaissance offices in Stonybrook, New York, felt like Caltech, not a hedge fund. If you worked at Renaissance, in addition to working in a very unique and cool environment, there was a good chance you would be very wealthy, since you had the chance to invest in Medallion. There was nothing like it, and may never be again.

By late June, I had taken a trip to the Renaissance offices in Stonybrook for the day and spent time with all the senior people at the firm. The only problem was that Jim was on vacation and he wanted to talk to me in person before we made a decision. He was on a boat off the coast of Sicily and wasn't returning anytime soon, so he came up with a plan: Anthony and I would fly to Amsterdam. Jim would arrange a plane to take us from Amsterdam to Palermo, Sicily. We would then be picked up by a private boat near Palermo and taken to his yacht, which was cruising off the Aeolian Islands near Sicily. Not too shabby. Jim's boat, the *Archimedes,* is 220 feet long, one of the largest private ships in the world. The *Archimedes* had only been finished that spring of 2008. We would stay a few days with Jim and his family and then make our plans from there if we wanted to stay in Italy or fly back. How cool was this? Yachting in the Tyrrhenian Sea on one of the world's most beautiful private boats. I mean it was really Brad and Angelina–type stuff. Except for the hedge fund job, of course.

You're not going to like this, but I turned down the trip. I opted out of what would probably have been the most luxurious and unique experience of our lives. Anthony would have loved to have gone, but he understood. Why did I not go? Because it became clear to me I couldn't take the job, and it didn't seem right to go if I really knew that. The job description included a tremendous amount of travel, particularly in Asia and the Middle East. That should have been fine, since I had spent at least the last dozen years of my career traveling constantly for work, so I knew the drill. But when I thought about constant work travel at that point, something had changed. Even though I couldn't see the bigger transformation coming yet, it no longer seemed exciting to be getting on the next flight and arriving in the next city. Anthony had come into my life, my priorities were shifting, and the Renaissance job wasn't going to work for me. That doesn't sound like the person who wanted to get right back in the game. I was obviously conflicted.

The Renaissance job offer is probably the best job offer I ever got in finance. But it wasn't for the Erin Version 2.0. Even though I wasn't totally aware that this seismic shift was happening inside of my psyche, my actions were an indicator. It ultimately took me much longer to realize the change in myself more completely, but the hints were there. You may think I was a little hardheaded if I didn't figure it out when I skipped the trip of a lifetime on Jim's boat and declined the job of a lifetime at Renaissance. If I know anything about myself, I know my head can be concrete. Sometimes nothing penetrates but a good jackhammer.

A few others could see my conflict, too. Just around the same time in late June that I was contemplating the Renaissance job, I spent the day interviewing with another old client, the highly successful hedge fund Citadel, in Chicago. I was thinking very seriously about how I could work out my life and have a senior job there. Chicago wasn't very practical, since I had lived in New York my whole life, but I tended to ignore those details if it meant a good job. I had a meeting with Adam Cooper, the general counsel, whom I had spent a good amount of time with over the prior few years. Early in our discussion he moved off point and asked me very directly, "Do you still have *it?* The drive? The confidence?" I was shocked. How could he ask that question when it was only two weeks after I'd resigned my position as CFO of a large investment bank under pretty dramatic circumstances? I was insulted. "Yes. That's why I'm here," I said. But Adam saw something I didn't see in myself yet. I didn't still have *it*. Not for that job and not for most other jobs. The change had overtaken me against my will. I just didn't know it yet.

Out of all the meetings, calls, lunches, and coffee klatches I had in June and July of 2008, no one else asked this question. No one else even suggested the possibility that I wasn't up for the next job, that something was broken in me. Anthony tried to slow me down. He didn't understand my sense of urgency. He had confidence in me and thought I should take six months and think long and hard about what I wanted to do next. But I don't think he fully appreciated how broken I was yet either. That would come a few months later, and it would be undeniable. He didn't get my rushing around on all the interviews so that only a month later I could announce that I had taken a senior job at Credit Suisse. He didn't get how desperately I need to make the case that I had bounced back. I was resilient. I had to convince myself of that version of the story, as imperfect as my methods turned out to be.

Ultimately, the path to the supposed redemption job at Credit Suisse was humorous at times. I went to the Credit Suisse building on lower Madison Avenue several times in late June and early July so I could meet with various people and we could all be comfortable that the job would be a good fit for me. After one day of interviews, Anthony picked me up from their offices and we drove out to East Hampton. We stopped at some point about halfway through the drive to pick up some provisions for the house. As we got back into the car, Anthony said, "You know what you're wearing is see-through, right?" "What? It's black. It's not see-through," I answered emphatically. I certainly would not wear see-through clothes to work. How crazy. "I'll take a picture of you in the light when we get to the house and you'll see," he countered confidently. I thought he was being a little hypercritical. Right after we got to the house, Anthony took a picture of me in the light of the kitchen and showed it to me triumphantly. And he was right! Oh my goodness! It wasn't like I wasn't wearing a bra and underwear, but the black fabric was pretty transparent in the bright light.

I was wearing a matching top and skirt from Chanel that I had never worn before. I had gotten dressed in my apartment that morning where I had large mirror in an interior hallway that had no natural light. That's where I would do my final check on my clothes before I left for work. I couldn't tell at all in that hallway light. Now, I was panicking. I started to rack my brain about whether I had been up and about during the several interviews I had at Credit Suisse that afternoon. Luckily, the more I thought about it, I had stayed pretty much sitting at a conference table and I hadn't been near a window. Maybe no one who had interviewed me had noticed, although I bet the receptionist and security people in the lobby did. After I accepted the Credit Suisse offer, Anthony would joke with me about my wardrobe choice for that day of interviews. "Of course they made you a good offer," he would say, "You were interviewed half naked! I would have definitely hired you! And for more money!" I still hope up until now that's our inside joke. Wishful thinking maybe.

But back to more serious matters. On July 15, the press release was issued by Credit Suisse, announcing that I was joining them to run their hedge fund business. Why the Credit Suisse job, with all the opportunities that were available? In the past, I had always been ready to move on, and the jobs my hedge fund clients were offering me would give me the chance to do something different. There were two reasons. First, I wasn't ready to bow out of the investment banking world. I liked working at a large organization and what that allowed you to do. Just because my tenure was cut short at Lehman didn't mean I was ready to exit that environment. Second, and really more importantly, there was someone at Credit Suisse whom I trusted to look out for me.

Rob Shafir, who was head of Credit Suisse in the Americas, had left Lehman in 2007. He had been the head of the equities business and a member of the Executive Committee until he was unceremoniously removed from that job by Joe Gregory, and left to suffer in limbo for around a year before his departure. That's when I got to know Rob. He was managing some of the senior hedge fund relationships and we overlapped when I took on the hedge fund banking job in 2006. We spent time together covering the hedge fund client base and he introduced me to many of the clients who ultimately became some my best relationships in the sector. Rob was and is a genuinely good and decent human being, and a person of remarkable character and ethics that seems to be very hard to find in big business these days. Even with the sense of misplaced trust and loyalty that I felt toward Dick and Joe in late June of 2008, I didn't give up on the idea that you needed someone to count on. To look out for you. I didn't want to fly blind into any of these jobs, build up my fortress, turn inward, and hope for the best. It was still overwhelmingly important to me to feel part of something I believed in, working with someone I trusted. That gave the Credit Suisse job a leg up on all the other possibilities. I took the job with confidence that Rob would have my back, and if other events hadn't interceded it all may have worked. Still, when things turned bad for me personally after only a few months on the job, Rob confirmed that he was the person I thought he was. He was a compassionate mentor and friend as I went through some darker days and my ultimate exit from Credit Suisse. At least some of my good instincts were still intact.

The Credit Suisse announcement was made in mid-July and I give myself six weeks to try to enjoy the summer until I started working again right after Labor Day. September 2, 2008, was the first day on the new job. And as I look at my calendar for those first two weeks it is a whirlwind of internal meetings and client meetings. I was the new kid on the block. I had a lot of catching up to do. Not even two weeks after I started at Credit Suisse, on September 14, Anthony and I first heard the story that Lehman was filing for bankruptcy. I had been completely and deliberately out of touch with anyone from Lehman since my final departure in June and I can't describe what a shock the bankruptcy news was. I could never have imagined that scenario. It seemed impossible that it could have come to that. As hard as it was for me to picture that life had gone on at 745 Seventh Avenue without me there, it was even harder to picture that life wouldn't go on there. I also had no clue what the personal ramifications would be to such an event. In the moment it seemed incredibly sad and disturbing. But somehow it all seemed very distant. I wasn't privy to how events had unfolded in the three months since I resigned the CFO job. I had worked hard that summer to shut out my thoughts about what had happened because I really didn't know what to think about it. Lehman had become something apart from myself. Its ups and downs were no longer mine. Or at least, that's what I thought.

It only took about ten days before the Lehman bankruptcy came knocking at my door. On Friday, September 26, 2008, two FBI agents came to Credit Suisse to personally hand me my first subpoena. Lucky for me, I was in a meeting and no one was quite sure where to find me in the building. One of the lawyers at Credit Suisse accepted the service on my behalf. I am trying to picture myself going down to the lobby to meet the agents and get the subpoena. I know I would have cried. I didn't yet understand that the bankruptcy would pull on me for the next six years. The Lehman I had loved, that I had been so devastated to leave, that I tried to put behind me, would now come to dominate my life again for years to come. Occasionally I would look up from my desk at Credit Suisse in those few months following the bankruptcy announcement look out to the trading floor and see my picture on the CNBC screens that were omnipresent throughout the floor. I had no idea what they were saying, but I would notice traders trying to discreetly look toward me to see if I had noticed. I had a meeting with one of my friendly hedge fund clients from AQR Capital Management in mid-October and I remember him asking me how I did it. "How are you functioning?" he said in a sympathetic manner. "I just have to," I replied simply. "What else can I do?"

But I really wasn't functioning very well. In fact, I wasn't functioning at all under my traditional definition of the word. Getting myself up each morning and entering the building on Madison Avenue was extremely painful, even with Anthony so thoughtfully walking me there each day. For me, the person who had loved strolling into the building at 745 Seventh Avenue with confidence and optimism, it felt awful to walk into the Madison Avenue offices of Credit Suisse with a sadness and lethargy that was a far cry from my old vigor. Not much good came from my working life in those few months until the end of the year in 2008, with one notable exception. Credit Suisse found for me an excellent lawyer. Bob Cleary, a former US Attorney, specialized in white collar crime at the law firm of Proskauer Rose in Manhattan. Bob would prove to be everything I could have hoped for in someone to represent me. He was an extremely talented lawyer coupled with being a genuinely compassionate and kind person. Although the focus of the Lehman legal experience morphed from criminal to civil investigations over time, Bob would always stay the point person with me. He still checks in with me regularly to see how I am doing. Most importantly, I always felt he really believed in me and my version of events. And in the end, I think nothing would have been more important than that. Later in the game, Al Pavlis of Finn Dixon & Herling would take on my representation. Al was also great; another good lawyer and kind to me. I couldn't have asked for more from these two gentlemen.

While I was dragging myself to my new job every day that fall of 2008, trying to jump-start a business effort and a presence, I was simultaneously starting to attend hours and hours of meetings with lawyers, prepping for my first official interview related to a criminal investigation by the State of New Jersey slated for December 30. My calendar was riddled with legal prep afternoon sessions, night sessions, whole-day sessions. Bob's team at Proskauer was fantastic, especially Dieter Snell and Mark Davidson, who, along with Bob, helped me through the next six years of our legal battle. But as good as they were, and as kind to me as they were, I was slowly crumbling. Each time I sat in their offices and reviewed events, people, e-mails, documents, a little part of me was eroding. I just kept thinking how all the hard work, sacrifices, and skill had led to this. I was being investigated as a criminal. I didn't know how to make any sense of how that fit into my view of how the world worked and what was important. I couldn't step outside of it and get any perspective. It seemed impossible that someday it would be over. That not all of it was a waste. That not every decision up until then had been the wrong one.

It wasn't just the damage to my professional reputation that was haunting me. The personal financial havoc that my short stint as CFO would wreak was just beginning to rear its ugly head. Until now, I have deliberately stayed away from the whole topic of money because it tended not to be a primary motivator for me. I cared about what I got paid because it was a benchmark of my performance, not because I wanted or needed more money. That was the key to it. It was all relative. And, importantly, given my chosen career path, I didn't have to worry about money. It was there. Money was a given as long as I was doing well at work. But the luxury of that way of thinking fell by the wayside when Lehman filed for bankruptcy.

As CFO, I was paid what would be considered a minimal amount of money for a corporate executive. Ultimately, I was paid about half a year's base salary. Your base salary at that level would be less than 10 percent of your total pay for the year, with your bonus making up the rest. When I walked out the door in that summer of 2008, I just left. I didn't wait around to get my bonus, which would have been almost all of my compensation for the year. I didn't hire a lawyer and negotiate a severance or exit package. There was no golden parachute. I just left.

Leaving that way had a huge financial penalty. But that was my decision. The imperative that drove me to leave wasn't exactly rational. I did what I felt I needed to do for my psychological well-being. I figured I would get another high-paying job quickly so I didn't worry about the money. But I should have taken better care in this regard. With the bankruptcy and my role as CFO, I have spent several times more than I was paid as CFO on lawyers and settlements in the past seven years. There was no walking away with boatloads of money. Not what anyone imagines, I am sure. The insurance that covered the litigation expenses for the executives eventually ran out and every legal and settlement expense after that was out of pocket. There were years when Anthony and I figured we might have to file for personal bankruptcy based on how things were progressing. It never came to that, but it was certainly possible, which was a completely unexpected reality. To lighten things up, Anthony would tease me that I could be in *Playboy* to make some money back. How could I not be flattered? In seriousness, though, all the effort and sacrifice to achieve professional excellence at the expense of every other aspect of my life led to reputational and nearly financial ruin? I guess you can see why I was questioning myself.

Even with Anthony by my side each morning, the few short blocks that was my journey to Credit Suisse was long and depressing.

A crisis of major proportions was building inside of me. I couldn't control it and I couldn't talk about it. As I got into mid-December and the meeting with the New Jersey investigators, I was cracking. A week later, on December 23, Anthony and I had spent the early part of the evening at a birthday dinner for one of his cousins on Long Island. We drove back to the house in East Hampton and at some point we had an argument. For the life of me, I can't remember the topic, but I was so out of sorts by that point I am sure it was my fault. I was depressed, sad, and angry all bundled up in one little firecracker ready to explode. I did. I went upstairs to our bedroom and looked around to find whatever I could. I wound up taking all the sleeping pills I had in the bottle. I don't remember anything else until I woke up the next morning in Southampton Hospital. It was the morning of Christmas Eve. Anthony was right by my side. It had been a terrible night for him. Finding me like that. Getting the ambulance. Standing vigil by my side at the hospital. Praying for me. Caring for me. My savior. My hero. How could I have done that to him? I have asked myself that so many times since then. It was so horribly wrong. So terribly selfish. There is never going to be an acceptable answer to that question.

Anthony always says to me that when you live a big life there are big consequences, both good and bad. Ain't that the truth. But after December 23, 2008, even I had to recognize that the story I thought I was living wasn't the right one. I wasn't going to be the "Comeback Kid." That notion was now completely inconceivable. I had to change my life and my priorities dramatically so that I would never again make a decision like the one I made the night of December 23. I think sometimes about what really would have happened if I'd been successful on that night. Whom I would have hurt, permanently and devastatingly. What I would have missed out on. It's so simple to see as I sit here with my beautiful, precious daughter. The tremendous happiness and peace I've felt in the most recent year of my life is a gift. I was ready to throw this great gift away. I didn't just think about discarding my life, I actually tried to. What I needed was a path back to a version of life that wasn't so fragile. A path toward resiliency and courage and confidence. The key was figuring out how to get there, and deciding whether I would insist on going it alone, as I'd always done. Would I accept help this time?

CHAPTER FIFTEEN

Starting Over

IN 2012, ABOUT A YEAR after Anthony and I started fertility treatments in hopes we could have a child together, we were back at the NYU Fertility Center already trying our third full round of an IVF cycle. Once again, we were there for the embryo transfer. A big day. The nurse walked us into the doctor's waiting room and said, "He'll be here in a minute." Anthony and I both looked at each other immediately. Four men and three women work in the practice. Was it going to be the same doctor from a year ago? It was only a one-in-six shot, but somehow we knew. It was him. The "I've seen worse" guy who liked to talk about Wall Street came in.

But this time, it was 180 degrees different. I didn't expect him to remember us, but he did. He said we had two embryos that looked very good and he wished us the best. He shook Anthony's hand, and as the doctor and I walked down the hall together this time, he says, "So how are things off the fast track? It looks like it agrees with you. You look very peaceful." And I was. And he was kind. He still had to mention all the books he'd read in which my name had appeared, as I lay on the operating table, but he said, "I think you did a great job. It must have been very hard."

As I sit here writing this after having a healthy and happy pregnancy and precious daughter, I think of him. It didn't happen that time—we persisted for two more years—but that's not really the point. The point is the doctor had managed to come full circle in a short time frame. He could see, feel, and sense something about me that told him that what he had discussed with me the first go-round was not my world any more. Not my focus. Not what I cared about.

If only I had been as quick to react to the change as the doctor had been. For me, it has taken years to really move on. In early 2009, I told Credit Suisse I couldn't return to work, and I really had no intention of returning to Wall Street, period. Sound a little dramatic and extreme? Maybe, but I knew in my heart this was the truth for me. After December 23 and the hell I had put Anthony through, I knew I couldn't go back. Still, it's one thing to know that a decision must be made, and another thing to live that decision. The void in my life hearkened back to quitting gymnastics as a child. Back then I took something out of my life deliberately and voluntarily, something that had been my obsessive focus and priority above all other things. In 1979, I'd had the great advantage of being a thirteen-year-old girl. I had only put seven years or so into gymnastics. As much as I missed the all-encompassing presence of the sport in my life, I worked to fill the void as quickly as possible with new life priorities. Starting high school helped. I wasn't repeating the same patterns every day in the same place. I learned to move on. I learned to start over. And I was comfortable that the decision was a good one. A decision I'd made on my own terms, with the timing I had chosen for myself.

If only I could have been as good at the transition thirty years later
when I left Wall Street, but so much more was invested at that point.
Even with changed life patterns and a move out to East Hampton to
get out of Manhattan, the change of scenery didn't accomplish what
I'd hoped. If I've learned anything over the six years since I made the
decision to leave it all behind, it's that just because you reject the old
way of living your life doesn't mean you immediately embrace the logical alternative. I spent years in no-man's-land. One of the most
common things Anthony would ask me over these past several years is
"Are you all in?" He would repeat the question over and over to me at
various moments. He had good reason to repeatedly ask me this question because I wasn't. I was "all out" of my prior life, but not "all in"
on my new one. I didn't know where I belonged. I didn't know who I
was.

Right around the time that I left Credit Suisse in early 2009, Anthony set up a meeting for me with a counselor, Gerry Moriarty. After
September 11, Anthony had been required, like other firefighters who
had experienced significant loss, to attend mandatory counseling pro-
vided by the FDNY. In Anthony's case, he had worked at a firehouse
in midtown Manhattan and lost virtually his entire company. It was a
devastating life experience that he lives with every day. I knew that if
Anthony thought it would be good for me to talk to this counselor,
then it probably would be. Gerry and I talked a lot in that session, and
I think he got a fair sense of what was happening with me at that
point and the emotions I was struggling with. What stays with me
most was that he said, "Erin, you know what you *do* is not who you
are." So simple. So obvious. But for me, it was completely false. The
way I looked at the world, what I *did* was the totality of who I *was*.
And if I wasn't doing *it*, then was I anybody really? Was there any

value to me without my job? Was there any identity? Any sense of purpose? And the very sad truth was no, at least not in my mind.

So here's my catch-22. I make this earth-shattering decision to leave my career in 2009. I couldn't possibly do it anymore. I couldn't even force myself to go through the motions. What I did on December 23 of 2008 was the best evidence to support that case. But I had no idea what else to do with myself. For years I'd had an overwhelming feeling that I was very good at something. Not just good, but arguably one of the best at what I did. The problem is, I wasn't doing that any longer, I was trying to live a more conventional life with traditional priorities of home and family and friends. I wasn't even so-so at that. Because I'd spent so many years focused on something else to the extreme, my skills at regular life seemed pathetic. And for years, every time I screwed up in this new life, a part of me used to wonder why I didn't just stick to what I was good at? I was a square peg in a round hole. I wasn't meant for this. There are a second lifetime of stories that fit that theme in the years after I left Wall Street. I used to tease Anthony that I was going to write a book entitled, *Work Was Easy*, because honestly that's how it felt. Work was so much easier. Work was where I'd excelled and real life was where I stumbled.

But now I'm different. I wish it hadn't taken all these years to be in this happier place. But I am there now, and that's what matters. Most importantly to me now, Anthony is there with me, right by my side. He is what really matters. Having our baby girl is what really matters. I feel productive. I am productive. It all should have been possible in one life. Having a great job, a husband I love, and children. If I had allowed room and time and put effort into all of these things I really think it would have been possible. I didn't. I didn't have to live my life in two such drastically different phases. It wasn't the best way, but I've found peace and happiness. Tragic events will still have the ability to shake me, but I've poured a new foundation that will allow me to weather the storms that will come.

At the end of 2013, I did get pregnant for the first time after all the rounds of IVF. Even better, I was pregnant with twins. Anthony and I were thrilled. It felt like finally, finally after the years, we had accomplished the unthinkable. But sadly for us, the twins didn't make it past ten weeks. I was devastated. We learned the bad news just before Thanksgiving. It hit me hard. I wasn't prepared for how strongly I would feel. It did shake me. I didn't handle it well. My immediate reaction was to give up, but that reaction faded fast. My next reaction was that we had to start right away again. Immediately. As soon as the doctors would let us. Our guardian angel at NYU, Dr. Elizabeth Fino, would help us through with sensitivity and good advice as she had each step of the way. And as is his style, Anthony counseled me to wait before trying again. Not rush back in to another round of IVF. To take our time. I listened to him and he was right. I needed to wait. We needed to wait as a couple. And with the waiting came some wisdom and some clarity. We decided in early 2014 that we would only do one more round of IVF and, if it didn't work out, we would move on with our lives. Put the IVF chapter behind us just as we had with so many other pieces of our lives. We loved each other and had a wonderful life together, even if a child wasn't meant to be part of it. There were children in our lives, albeit grown ones. I had two step-children, Anthony's children Kate and Anthony, that I cared about. We were a modern family. This was no sob story.

It's funny. I used to tell Anthony that if I got pregnant, I would change my last name. We were married in 2011, but somehow I thought it didn't really matter if I changed my name unless we had a child. I know even with children these days it's not necessary, and maybe in New York these days, not even conventional. But I did feel it would simplify things for our child. Two parents with the same last name. Why not make it easy on him or her? What did my name really mean at this point anyway? I wasn't planning on going back to my old career. What was I clinging to? Some last vestige of my old self? So after the miscarriage, when having a child seemed unlikelier than ever, I changed my name. It occurred to me that maybe I was putting the cart before the horse. But I thought, why wait to change my name until we had a baby? Why not change my name and see what happens? I know on some level this sounds ridiculous, but changing my last name felt like a dramatic step. The final change that would bring me full circle. Callan is my middle name, but Montella is my last name. For everything. It feels so right for me. I am no longer just the singular individual making my way in the world. Anthony and I do it together. As a team. We are joined as one in every way that I know. I did get pregnant after changing my name, so go figure. God works in mysterious ways.

As I have pointed in this new direction, all that came before these last six years has become more distant and less relevant. The emotion of it has waned. The significance of it seems small. How do I know for sure? I got a phone call in January of 2015 on my cell phone. I didn't recognize the number, which for years would have meant I wouldn't pick it up. I was always avoiding the press and hated to get stuck answering live. Eventually Anthony convinced me just to pick up these calls from unknown callers. Stop all the avoidance. "You can always say you have no comment," he would tell me. "Or, in the worst case, just hang up." Of course he's right. You can't really do anything to me across the phone lines. So I picked up. "Erin, are you sitting down?" a man asks me. A voice I am not sure if I know. I was sitting down. "Yes I am," I say tentatively. Now I was mad that Anthony told me to pick up these stupid calls from unknown numbers because God knows who this was going to be. "Erin, it's Dick Fuld." Dick Fuld. Dick Fuld! Six and a half years since I last spoke to him and he was calling me, just as I was finishing writing this memoir. Maybe we were on the same self-realization schedule? Maybe six years is the necessary minimum to figure things out. I don't know. But his timing was impeccable.

He said everything I had wanted to hear for so many years. He was sorry about what had happened to me. He felt he had left me on my own to handle things and shouldn't have. It wasn't fair. It wasn't right. And still after all this time he felt he'd made the right decision to choose me for the CFO job. That I was the best person to be CFO and he never thought anything else. There was a fair amount more to it, but that was the gist of it. I told him about my marriage with Anthony and that I was only a few weeks from having a baby, and he seemed genuinely happy about that, and that I had found a new purpose and fulfillment in life. He understood why I'd left Wall Street, even if he'd chosen not to. It felt strange to be having such a serious and personal conversation with him, but that was the nature of it.

If you are surprised to learn of this call, imagine my surprise. Once I got past the fact that Dick had called, two things really struck me about our conversation. One is that I give Dick all the credit in the world for calling me. That was a very hard phone call to make, and at that late date it didn't need to be made. But he felt compelled to make it and that encourages me to believe on some level that I hadn't been so wrong in my estimation of him years before. Only a decent person with a conscience makes that kind of a phone call. He doesn't run into me. I don't live in his world, nor does he live in mine. We may never have occasion to see each other again, but he wanted to call and let me know that he felt accountable. That he felt bad.

The second thing that struck me about this call was how much it didn't matter to me. I don't say that to undermine everything I just said. I say that because it wasn't a life-changing event. You'd think I would have waited all these years for an apology. For Dick or Joe to say they were sorry. When it finally came you, would think it would be cathartic. But it was the distant past. All the emotions that went along with the end of my career were no longer raw and at the surface. The desperate and dramatic behavior that drove me to the night of December 23, 2008, had long disappeared, along with that crazy way I had of looking at the world and living my life. It had been replaced by a life that was more in balance. More secure. So as much as I appreciated the call, and I genuinely did, I put it in its proper place. A final closing for that chapter of my life, leaving it with a better ending. The loose ends tied up. It gave me more confidence that I was not alone in trying to start over and make things right.

And remarkably I am still here. I feel like one of my rosebushes. I cut them all the way down in the spring. It doesn't feel like the right time. I feel bad doing it as I see how stubby and sad-looking they are when I've finished. I can't imagine they will actually grow enough to compensate when summer really kicks in. Then they grow back bigger and more beautiful than ever. It always surprises me. I was cut to the quick in 2008, seemingly in the prime of my career, and now I'm happier and more complete these several years later. Although I never envisioned this outcome, I have Anthony and my beautiful baby girl, Maggie. I will have the chance as her mother, with Anthony, to guide our daughter as she navigates her life and all the competing priorities.

She will grow up so many years after me, but, I think, with all the same pitfalls, possibilities, and challenges. Because figuring out what really matters to you and how it dictates the direction of your time, your energy, your passion is always at the heart of the matter. She will have our guidance and support, but ultimately she will decide for herself and she will always know my story.

ERIN CALLAN WAS THE CHIEF financial officer of Lehman Brothers and a member of its Executive Committee during the height of the financial crisis from late 2007 until mid-2008. Prior to holding the CFO position, she held various business head positions over a dozen years throughout the now defunct investment bank. Erin was a corporate tax lawyer at Simpson Thacher & Bartlett, a New York-based law firm for five years prior to joining Lehman Brothers in 1995. Erin graduated *magna cum laude* from Harvard College in 1987 and thereafter received a law degree from NYU Law School in 1990.

Erin's tenure as CFO of Lehman Brothers extended through the Bear Stearns collapse and ended prior to Lehman's bankruptcy filing. She was the public face of Lehman during this tumultuous period and her role was widely covered by the media both at the time and in the aftermath of the crisis. She was recognized in 2007 as a "Woman to Watch" by *Fortune Magazine* in their annual review of the "Most Powerful Women in Business" and the *Wall Street Journal*. The *New York Post* ranked her as the third most powerful woman in New York in 2008.

Erin grew up In Douglaston, New York, a neighborhood in Queens. She is married to Anthony Montella and has a daughter, Margaret Mary Montella.

Made in the USA
San Bernardino, CA
31 March 2016